Design Your Own Wedding Ceremony

The late Michael Perry was a Canon of Rochester Cathedral and the Vicar of Tonbridge Parish Church in Kent. He was a recognized authority on contemporary worship and a member of the Jubilate group, which has produced numerous worship resources. His previous books include *The Wedding Book*, *Preparing for Worship*, *The Dramatized Bible* and *Bible Prayers for Worship*. This book was in preparation at the time of his death in 1996.

Rowena Edlin-White graduated in English and Drama and spent a number of years working in the theatre and in television. She is a freelance writer specializing in gender issues and a published poet and children's author. She is also a licensed Reader in the Church of England.

Design Your Own Wedding Ceremony

MICHAEL PERRY &
ROWENA EDLIN-WHITE

Marshall Pickering
An Imprint of HarperCollinsPublishers

Marshall Pickering is an Imprint of
HarperCollins*Religious*
Part of HarperCollins*Publishers*
77–85 Fulham Palace Road
London W6 8JB

First published in Great Britain
in 1997 by Marshall Pickering

1 3 5 7 9 10 8 6 4 2

A catalogue record for this book is
available from the British Library

0 551 030240

Printed and bound in Great Britain by
Caledonian International Book Manufacturing Ltd,
Glasgow

Contents

Introduction

The fact that you have picked up this book is already some indication that you would like your wedding to be something more than just a set formula with 'all the usual things'. You are probably looking for some ideas on how to personalize your special day and want to know what is allowed where, and what choices are on offer.

Perhaps you feel you don't fit the mould of 'the average young couple' and want to explore alternatives which might suit you better. You will need to know who to approach and where to look to achieve the particular kind of ceremony you want.

Every wedding is special; it is a public declaration of your commitment to one another and an opportunity to express the hopes and desires you have for a long-lasting relationship. This book should go some way in helping you create a unique event which will say something about you both and your aspirations for your life together, as you celebrate your marriage in the presence of your family and friends.

Rowena Edlin-White

1

The Right Wedding for You

You've decided to get married – congratulations!
Before long it will begin to dawn on you both that
there are umpteen practicalities to consider, and
important arrangements to make. Some decisions will
be influenced by your particular circumstances (where
you live, for example, or whether you have been married
before), other things are a matter of personal taste. So give
yourselves plenty of time to think through what kind of
wedding is right for you.

What kind of wedding do you want?

Do you want a big, lavish affair with your friends and
family and all the trimmings? Or would you rather have a
quiet ceremony with just a few people? Do you see your
wedding as an affirmation of a relationship that already
exists – you may have shared a home for some time and
even have children – or do you want it to be a significant
start to something new, the beginning of a new life together?
Finance may be a contributing factor in this matter. Are
your parents paying for the wedding? If they are, it is likely
they will expect some say in the proceedings. Alternatively,

1

are you organizing and paying for the whole event yourself? If so, then you know the limits of your resources and will also be able to exercise more control over the arrangements. Where will you get married – a register office or a church? And if a church, which denomination?

All these are the sort of questions worth discussing together before deciding upon your choice of venue and approaching your chosen minister or registrar. The venue, participants, prayers, readings and music can all contribute to the flavour of the day. Dare to be different! When planning your wedding, consider all aspects from the wording of the invitations to the reception; especially, though, think carefully about that bit in the middle which is the reason for it all. Every part of your day can say something about what you believe and how you see your relationship. If there are things which really matter to you but the local vicar isn't prepared to let you have them, obviously you want to know right at the beginning so that you can consider a compromise or go elsewhere. So make sure to leave yourselves plenty of time to organize it – at least three months.

And be warned! If you are thinking of doing anything at all out of the ordinary, somebody will be offended or disagree – it is inevitable! Whilst it may be prudent to compromise on some things it is, after all, your day, and it is worth sticking out for what you want.

A Christian wedding

There is, of course, nothing to stop you marrying in a civil ceremony (in a register office), and then having a service of dedication somewhere totally different (on a beach, in a hot-air balloon), led by anyone you like, and expressing your own particular beliefs. For the purposes of this book, however, we will assume that – for whatever reason, whether regular church-goers or not – you would like some Christian element in your wedding, based on a Christian marriage service. (See page 156 for a list of useful books that offer lots of unusual ideas for those that don't aspire to a Christian viewpoint.)

One of the first decisions to make is where you will get married. Brainstorm a few ideas about the sort of wedding you want and skim through some of the later chapters in this book to help you decide.

Where will you get married?

This will depend to some extent on the kind of wedding you would like and how persistent you are prepared to be to achieve it. Nowadays in England you need not be restricted to a church or register office; weddings may take place in hotels, National Trust properties and other venues, as long as they have the requisite licence, a minister is willing to perform the ceremony, and a registrar is present. One thing to remember is that in England it is the *building* that is licensed for marriages, in Scotland the *minister*, so in theory you have more choice north of the border!

Register Offices

Register offices are much pleasanter places than they used to be; the registrar usually does his or her best to make sure the ceremony is personal for you. Bear in mind that the service is, of necessity, brief and to the point (about 20 minutes) and has no religious content: it is a legal service for everybody. However, many registrars allow minor changes so long as they don't alter the legal requirements or

3

lengthen the proceedings. For example, some will let you take in your own taped music, or have prose or poetic readings, so long as they have no religious connotations (that includes the titles of the pieces). For some ideas as to what to choose see Chapter 7. If you do want to include some kind of spiritual expression in the service, then perhaps a blessing service in a church afterwards would be suitable.

For a register office marriage you need either a Certificate, or a Certificate and Licence. If both of you have been resident in one registration district of England or Wales for seven days immediately before giving notice of your intending marriage, a Certificate will suffice. If you live in different registration districts, notice must be given in both. The Certificate will be issued a minimum of 21 clear days later.

To marry by Certificate and Licence, one of you must have lived in a registration district of England or Wales for 15 days prior to giving notice. The Licence can then be issued after one clear day. You only have to give one notice if you are getting married by Certificate and Licence even if you both live in different districts. This method is more expensive but does allow you to get married sooner.

You will also, of course, need to give notice of marriage at your local Register Office if you are getting married in any other church or venue apart from the Church of England.

Churches

In England, Anglican churches (the Church of England) are automatically licensed for marriages. Anyone has a right to be married in their local Anglican church, providing they or their partner live in the parish or are on the electoral roll of the church in question (though residential qualifications are currently being reviewed and this could soon change).

Note, however, that the Church in Wales, the Church of Ireland and the Episcopal Church of Scotland – which are its close relatives – do not have the same arrangement.

Other churches and chapels of other denominations have their own arrangements and in some cases a registrar is required to be present. Roman Catholics have their own rules about who may or may not marry in a Catholic church, so if one or both of you has a Catholic background, a call to your local priest should confirm whether or not you are eligible.

Banns/Licences

In the case of the Church of England, banns or notice of intention to marry must be read out during a church service on three consecutive occasions. If you live in different parishes to one another, the banns must be read in both parish churches; in addition, if you are marrying in a third church where one or both of you are members on the electoral roll, banns must be read there also. Check with your minister about this. Special licences granted by the Archbishop of Canterbury are sometimes issued which allow you to marry in a church other than your parish church; in this case, banns do not need to be read and the marriage can take place at any time. If you are in a hurry, marriage by Common Licence is an alternative; the local diocesan council issues this and it is valid for three months. Consult with your vicar if either of the two aforementioned suggestions seems applicable.

If you opt for a church of another denomination, for example, Methodist, Baptist, Congregationalist, United Reformed, Assemblies of God, etc., do contact the minister in charge as usual; although Nonconformist wedding services are similar to the Church of England, they often have much more flexibility and are likely to be open to

5

innovation. The minister will tell you what you have to do to begin the process of obtaining a licence.

What if you have been married before?

Whilst there is no problem in a register office, if one or both of you have been divorced, it may affect the church and/or type of ceremony available to you. In many cases, there are no hard and fast rules and you will just have to enquire as to what particular line is taken by the church of your choice. Some guidelines follow, but it may be better to list several possibilities and work through them, steeling yourselves for a disappointment or two along the way.

Roman Catholic

All marriages which take place in a Catholic church or – for a serious reason – elsewhere (for example, in hospital), are seen as valid unless or until proved otherwise. Neither party in a valid Catholic marriage is free to re-marry in a Catholic church unless their partner has died or the marriage has been annulled. This applies also to non-Catholics seeking to marry Catholics, so if either of the two parties requesting a Catholic marriage is already joined in what is seen by the Church as a valid marriage, that marriage must first be annulled. Civil divorce does not equal annulment.

Church of England

There are no hard and fast rules within the Anglican Church, although some priests may feel they cannot in all conscience marry a divorced person or persons. However, many are more than willing to do so, sometimes after consultation with a local board of reference. If you are prepared to settle for a service of blessing, most Anglican priests will be happy to oblige (see Chapter 3).

Baptist

Guidelines vary from church to church. Some may not marry people who are divorced. However, others will sometimes make exceptions for people who have subsequently become Christians. This policy is founded on the basis of 2 Corinthians 5:17: 'If anyone is in Christ they are a new creation; the old has gone, the new has come!'

In such cases, the couple must usually provide evidence of their Christian faith. Policy will differ from one Baptist church to another because it is based on the decision of the whole congregation.

Methodist

The Methodist Church recognizes that although marriage as a life-long union is the ideal, for a variety of reasons a marriage may break down irretrievably. Officially, anyone can be remarried in a Methodist church; however, a couple usually have to show that they have a commitment to the Christian faith and some connection with that particular church. If they don't, they may be asked to make one. Again, policies vary with different churches and ministers; it may be sufficient that one of your parents is a member there.

United Reformed Church

Individual ministers have the discretion to act without consulting anyone else when deciding to give a couple permission to remarry, unless there is a local agreement to

7

consult with other ministers. No minister can be made to act against their conscience. How much insistence is placed on the couple's attendance at worship and how deeply their faith may be questioned will also vary according to the particular minister or church.

Society of Friends or Quakers

Quaker Faith & Practice 1994 states that they '... should be sympathetic to and understanding of those who have been divorced ... [and] are given discretion whether or not to grant permission to those who wish to re-marry in a Friends' Meeting' (6.17).

Don't give up!

It is hurtful to be told you cannot be married in the church of your choice either because of residential regulations or for reasons of previous marriage breakdown, especially if you are the innocent party. Try not to take it personally; the priest or minister may have serious problems of conscience about remarriage, or their hands may be tied by that particular Church's tradition or policy. If you want a church wedding, persevere! Somewhere there is a church prepared to welcome you and marry you.

When can you get married?

The Church of England (along with its Irish, Welsh and Scottish cousins) tends to own old, rather picturesque, buildings which are immensely popular in June, July and August, when three or four weddings may follow one another on a single afternoon. If you want the time and space to do something different, choose a date outside 'the season'; in this way you don't have to hurry and the clergy are not so pushed to get you married and out of the church as quickly as possible! Just after Easter is a good time, or in the New Year. Fewer people are going for a Saturday wedding these days, for obvious reasons; so, if convenient, choose a weekday. You may, if you want, marry on a Sunday (usually in the afternoon, to fit in with regular Sunday services); this can be more leisurely and, on a practical note, parking will be easier – especially in town centres. The minister is likely to be more amenable if not anticipating a rush.

Setting the ball rolling

Ring the vicar or priest-in-charge of the parish church you would like to be married in; the number should be on the notice board. Tell him or her where you live, what your circumstances are (whether one of you has been married before, for example), and arrange to meet. You can then discuss what you have in mind and ask whether he or she is willing to let you do it. If not, look elsewhere.

Most clergy will subsequently arrange to see you again at least once before the big day. They may ask you to take part in some form of marriage preparation, either just the two of you, or with other couples. You may also be asked to attend the church you have chosen a number of times before the wedding; if it is an Anglican church, to hear your banns read. This is not a legal requirement but can be a pleasurable countdown to the wedding. Often a short prayer will be offered for couples about to get married, which gives a lovely sense of support from the whole congregation.

Visiting the church also gives you the opportunity to become familiar with its layout, what facilities there are (toilets or kitchen, for example), and what might or might not be appropriate for the service. For example, some churches don't have a central aisle, so don't plan an elaborate procession! Get a feel for the place. The churchwarden or superintendent will be happy to answer your questions. Ask to borrow a copy of the hymn book they use, as it will make things easier if the hymns you choose are readily available. Introduce yourselves to the organist or choir leader if you anticipate needing their services. Personal contact early on will help ensure good communication when it comes to choosing your music. A word with the person who organizes the flowers would also be in order, especially if you would like their co-operation on the day.

Don't be shy! Everybody likes a wedding and you are sure to receive a warm welcome.

2

The Wedding Ceremony

Background and history

The wedding ceremony – as we know it today – is relatively modern, although there have always been ceremonies in different cultures to mark the creation of a new family group. In the past, and still in some communities, the emphasis was as much upon the exchange of dowries and property between the two families as on the relationship of the two people involved. In Britain, the remnants of this may be seen in the custom of the bride being 'given away' and the groom asking the bride's father for permission to marry her, neither of which carry the significance they once did.

In some parts of the world, the betrothal or engagement was the crucial part of the act, and was considered binding. In many communities no ceremony of any kind took place and a couple became recognized as common-law husband and wife with the passage of time; interestingly, this seems to be gaining popularity once again as more couples opt to cohabit rather than marry. The declaration of intention to marry before witnesses was quite sufficient until a few centuries ago; then marriage became a church affair rather than a domestic affair, and the modern marriage service came into existence around the sixteenth century.

The exchange of rings or other precious articles to mark the marriage contract is an ancient custom, but brides didn't dress up in elaborate white gowns until Queen Victoria chose to do so for her own wedding, and there is no reason whatever why this should be adhered to. Many a bride would have invested in no more than a new bonnet, preferring to spend what savings she had on household items. The 'marriage industry' today is largely fired by commercial gain, urging you to spend thousands of pounds, whereas the actual marriage ceremony (whether in a church or a register office) costing under £200 is still the cheapest part of the whole proceedings.

The service: traditional or contemporary?

In what is now thought of as the traditional English wedding, the two families sit on opposite sides of the church and the groom hovers nervously at the front with his best man. The bride arrives last of all, to a great fanfare. She is accompanied by her bridesmaids, and walks up the aisle on the arm of a male relative who subsequently gives her away; whilst appearing queen of the day, she is generally the passive party. Many brides find that difficult to go along with nowadays and there are plenty of alternatives. But it is the spoken part of the service, where the couple commit themselves to one another before witnesses, which is the nub of the whole business – irrespective of the colour scheme, the cost of the dress, or anything else. The couple, in effect, marry themselves before God with the help of the minister, and the event is a mixture of solemnity and celebration.

What form of service shall we use?

Church of England

If marrying in an Anglican church you might want to use the traditional prayer book service (from the *Book of Common Prayer*), with all its 'thees' and 'thous' and readings from the King James Bible, together with some stately organ music and all the pomp and circumstance of a Victorian wedding. Surprisingly, this 'traditional' service is no longer universal: you will probably have to make a special request to use it. The version offered will be called 'The Form of Solemnization of Matrimony, Alternative Services, First Series'. It is not 'better' or more authentic, but it does have great dignity.

The more usual service is from the *Alternative Service Book* (ASB), called simply 'The Marriage Service' (1980). This uses modern language and makes concessions to contemporary society. For example, when the *Book of Common Prayer* (BCP) was written (in the seventeenth century) it was assumed that the bride owned no property of her own and only the groom had anything to give; this is therefore reflected in the BCP service. But in the ASB version both partners bestow 'all their worldly goods' upon each other. Today's bride is not required to 'obey' her husband either, unless she wants to; both services have an alternative passage.

You might like to compare the introductions to the two different services:

'The Form of Solemnization of Matrimony', Book of Common Prayer

Dearly beloved, we are gathered here in the sight of God and in the face of this congregation, to join together this man and this woman in Holy Matrimony; which is an honourable estate, instituted of God himself, signifying unto us the mystical union that is betwixt Christ and his Church; which holy estate Christ adorned and beautified with his presence, and first miracle that he wrought, in Cana of Galilee, and is commended in Holy Writ to be honourable among all men; and therefore is not by any to be enterprised, nor taken in hand, unadvisedly, lightly, or wantonly; but reverently, discreetly, soberly, and in the fear of God, duly considering the causes for which Matrimony was ordained.

First, It was ordained for the increase of mankind according to the will of God, and that children might be brought up in the fear and nurture of the Lord, and to the praise of his holy Name.

Secondly, It was ordained in order that the natural instincts and affections, implanted by God, should be hallowed and directed aright; that those who are called of God to this estate, should continue therein in pureness of living.

Thirdly, It was ordained for the mutual society, help, and comfort, that the one ought to have of the other, both in prosperity and adversity.

Into which holy estate these two persons present come now to be joined.

Therefore if any man can shew any just cause, why they may not lawfully be joined together, let him now speak, or else hereafter for ever hold his peace.

14

'The Marriage Service', Alternative Service Book

We have come together in the presence of God, to witness the marriage of N and N, to ask his blessing on them, and to share in their joy. Our Lord Jesus Christ was himself a guest at a wedding in Cana of Galilee, and through his Spirit he is with us now.

The Scriptures teach us that marriage is a gift of God in creation and a means of his grace, a holy mystery in which man and woman become one flesh. It is God's purpose that, as husband and wife give themselves to each other in love throughout their lives, they shall be united in that love as Christ is united with his Church.

Marriage is given, that husband and wife may comfort and help each other, living faithfully together in need and in plenty, in sorrow and in joy. It is given, that with delight and tenderness they may know each other in love, and through the joy of their bodily union, may strengthen the union of their hearts and lives. It is given, that they may have children and be blessed in caring for them and bringing them up in accordance with God's will, to his praise and glory.

In marriage husband and wife belong to one another, and they begin a new life together in the community. It is a way of life that all should honour; and it must not be undertaken carelessly, lightly, or selfishly, but reverently, responsibly, and after serious thought.

This is the way of life, created and hallowed by God, that N and N are now to begin. They will each give their consent to the other; they will join hands and exchange solemn vows, and in token of this they will give and receive a ring.

Therefore, on this their wedding day we pray with them, that, strengthened and guided by God, they may fulfil his purpose for the whole of their earthly life together.

Both are basically saying the same thing, although the language of the first is still rather archaic, despite some modernization. Will your guests understand it? Both emphasize that marriage is a life-long partnership for mutual comfort and support, which should not be undertaken lightly but after serious thought. The ASB dwells more on the mutuality of the partnership with a healthy affirmation of sexuality, whilst the updated BCP still maintains the belief that marriage is first and foremost for the procreation of children and the avoidance of immorality. Both refer to Jesus' attendance at the wedding in Cana where he turned the water into wine (John 2): he is assumed to be present at your wedding, whatever language you decide to use.

You can obtain booklets of both services from a Christian bookshop for a small sum (see page 156 for suggested useful books) or an ordinary bookshop will be able to order them for you. If in doubt, buy both and read them through carefully before you make a final decision.

Other churches

Many Nonconformist churches have no set marriage service but what they offer is very similar to the Anglican model. Here is an alternative introduction from the United Baptist Church of USA:[1]

A wedding is that occasion when a man and a woman publicly proclaim their love and declare their commitment to one another. By its very nature it is both a solemn and a happy event. For some of you gathered here, this ceremony will prompt a flood of personal memories, for others of you it will set in motion dreams and aspirations.

1. From *The Wedding Ceremony*, Revd John W. Bartol.

For all of us it will be a sharing in a most intimate and love-filled moment in the lives of two people we know and appreciate. But for __ and __, who stand here before us, this ceremony will be an act of participation in what they believe to be God's will for their lives.

By your presence here today you signify your interest in encouraging __ and __ in the new relationship into which they are about to enter. You are called upon to rejoice in their happiness, to be patient when they make mistakes, to help them in times of trouble and to remember them in your prayers.

God established marriage so that man and woman might have life-long companionship, that natural instincts and affections might be fulfilled in mutual love, that children might have the benefit of family life, and that society might rest on a firm foundation. The Apostle Paul compared married love to Christ's love for His Church. Thus he gave us a new vision of what marriage ought to be, a life of self-giving love.

The text above places the marriage firmly within the community, not as an isolated unit. Individual churches will probably have some basic words which you can ask to see, and Methodist and Baptist churches are normally happy to construct a service to suit you, so long as the service fulfils the legal requirements, is approved by the minister and includes a statement – such as the above – about Christian marriage.

The Quakers' form of service contains the bare minimum: the marriage takes place during the usual Quaker meeting which is predominantly silent. Early in the proceedings the couple stand and declare their intention to be married, saying:

Friends, I take this my friend __ to be my husband/wife, promising, through divine assistance (*or* with God's help) to be unto him/her a loving and faithful wife/husband, so long as we both on earth shall live (*or* until it shall please the Lord by death to separate us).

No changes to the wording other than those indicated above may be used. There is no minister and no exchange of rings. The marriage is registered, then the meeting continues as normal, mainly in silence. You don't both have to be members of the Society to be married in a Friends meeting but you will be expected to be in sympathy with Quaker beliefs; meetings for 'clearness' may be called 'to explore the nature of the commitment that is being contemplated' (*Quaker Faith & Practice 1994*, 16.17). The utter simplicity of the proceedings may be just what you are looking for.

In a Roman Catholic Church, if a baptized Catholic is marrying another baptized Christian (of any denomination) they may choose their order of service from either a Nuptial Mass or the standard Rite of Marriage; unless both parties are baptized Catholics the latter is normally used, as is the case if one party is not a baptized Christian. The couple may choose Bible readings, hymns and Bidding Prayers from the Rite of Marriage and will probably be allowed an additional, appropriate, non-biblical reading if they wish. They are also free to choose the organ music they would like.

Marriage in the context of a Eucharistic service

As mentioned above, a Roman Catholic wedding may take place in the setting of a Nuptial Mass, and an Anglican wedding or service of blessing may also, on request, include Holy Communion. Sometimes only bride and groom take communion; although this does speed things up a bit, it is not really in the spirit of the Communion Service which is, literally, for the whole community present. However, it might be appropriate if bride and groom are communicants (confirmed in the Church of England) and it is of deep significance to them, but the majority of the guests are not. If communion is offered for the whole congregation, do consider whether non-Christian family and friends might feel excluded. One way round this would be for the priest to invite all to come forward, to receive communion if appropriate or, if not, for a blessing.

Legal requirements

These are the parts of the service without which no marriage is valid. The witnesses present are asked to speak if they know any reason why the couple may not marry, then bride and groom are also asked if they know of 'any lawful impediment' to their marriage. They then consent to take one another as husband and wife and promise to remain together for the rest of their lives. The officiant then publicly pronounces them husband and wife and they sign the official register. This is the same formula whether in church, chapel or register office and may not be altered.

Parts which may be changed

In a church service, the couple also make certain vows or promises to remain together through the good times and the bad, and rings are blessed and exchanged as a symbol of 'unending love', as the ASB puts it. They then receive a blessing from the minister; prayers and a sermon or address then follows.

The ASB marriage service

Generally speaking, in the Church of England, sections 6–19 of the ASB marriage service – beginning with the Introduction and ending with the Blessing – are obligatory and must stand as written, though there is space for the odd tweak here and there! Vows, prayers, readings and music are dealt with in the following chapters but it is worth commenting on the standard Anglican service here:

Introduction

This is meant to be a general statement about marriage, not about yours in particular, but your minister might agree to leave out the part about children in paragraph 3 if you can't, in all conscience, go along with it. (See page 15.)

To obey or not to obey?

The ASB provides an alternative where both agree just to love and to cherish; in the original version, the bride obeys but the groom also promises to worship her in return. This might be thought a very fair exchange! You might consider leaving out 'obey' and 'worship' but inserting 'serve', which is another good biblical precept, in their place, if the minister agrees.

The rings

There is provision for one or two rings to be used. In recent years it has become fashionable once again for men to wear wedding rings, but it is up to you what you decide. For additional symbolic actions see Chapter 5.

The pronouncement

It might seem a small matter, but the Church in general is improving in its use of inclusive language. So if you don't like using 'men' and 'mankind' when it really means 'men and women' and 'people', say so. There's no reason why the minister shouldn't say: 'That which God has joined together let no one divide', rather than 'let no man divide'.

Other denominations

Nonconformist churches, whilst being obliged to fulfil the legal requirements, generally have more leeway as to what actual words are used; the minister will have his or her own flavour of introduction and may include your own suggestions. Vows, prayers, readings and blessings may also be expanded upon.

The address

Some kind of sermon or address is usual in a church service. You can leave it to the priest or minister to say a few encouraging words about marriage in general, or it might be done by someone else. You may have a friend who is a Christian minister, chaplain or elder from another church who could offer something more personal. It should be someone who will offer a Christian perspective, not a secular speech – the reception is the place for that! Ask permission from the officiating minister.

Involving your children

If you already have children, it is a good thing to try to involve them, acknowledging that this is the founding of a new family as much as the marriage of two people, and a big step for them too. In their book *Human Rites*, Hannah Ward and Jennifer Wild have included 'A ceremony for recognizing children during the wedding ceremony', in which the children are each presented with a medallion as a token of the shared bond which has been formed with the parents as a result of the marriage. The United Reformed Church also involves children in the promises (see Chapter 4 for both of these texts). If your children are old enough to know what they are doing, they could be your witnesses in church or in a civil ceremony; there is no official minimum age, but 13 or 14 is a suitable guideline, depending on the maturity of the child.

3

A Service of Blessing

You may decide, for all sorts of reasons, to opt for a service of blessing after a civil ceremony: one or both of you may have been married before and feel a church wedding is either impractical or inappropriate; you may come from different religious traditions; or you may have been married for some time already but feel this is the time to bring your marriage before God for dedication and blessing – there is no time limit, so far as I know! Although it is not a marriage service, there is no reason why the event should not be very special; indeed, there is perhaps more space for individual touches.

Because a service of blessing is not a legal ceremony you have more choice as to how and where it takes place. If you can persuade your priest or minister, it could take place in your own home, in a garden, by the river or in any church or chapel, with permission. Banns do not have to be read or licences obtained, though of course you will have to book the church in advance and give yourselves time to send out invitations if you want family and friends to be present. You may be able to organize everything so that you go straight from the civil ceremony to the church, as happens in many continental countries, where the two parts of the wedding are separate anyway. An alternative is to have the blessing in the context of an ordinary service, if you regularly attend a local church and, as with a wedding service, the service of blessing may have a Eucharist setting if the couple are both communicants.

Church of England

Different areas of the country do things in different ways, it depends on the guidelines set by the individual bishops. There is, however, a printed service available called 'Services of Prayer and Dedication after Civil Marriage' which has been approved for use. The prefatory notes are as follows:

The nature of the service

The service is one in which the couple – already married – wish to dedicate to God their life together. Because it is not a marriage service, banns may not be called nor any entry made in the Register of Marriages.

There need not be a procession into church; the couple usually enter together at the beginning and sit at the front. The Introduction speaks of marriage as being for mutual comfort and support of the couple, similar to the marriage service, but of course no witnesses are called nor legal declarations made because they are already married. One or two readings are used, hymns are sung, prayers offered, and a sermon preached. Instead of vows the couple dedicate themselves to one another:

The dedication

Minister: N and N, you have committed yourselves to
each other in marriage,
and your marriage is recognized by law.
The Church of Christ understands marriage to be, in the
will of God,
the union of a man and a woman,
for better, for worse,
for richer, for poorer,
in sickness and in health,
to love and to cherish,
till parted by death.
Is this your understanding of the covenant and promise
that you have made?

Husband and Wife: It is.

The minister says to the husband: N, have you resolved to
be faithful to your wife,
forsaking all others,
so long as you both shall live?

Husband: That is my resolve, with the help of God.

The minister says to the wife: N, have you resolved to be
faithful to your husband,
forsaking all others,
so long as you both shall live?

Wife: That is my resolve, with the help of God.

The rings

There is no giving and receiving of rings but the rings may be blessed as symbols of 'unending love and faithfulness'.

The minister then says to the people:
N and N have here affirmed their Christian
understanding and resolve in marriage
which they have begun. Will you their relatives
and friends do all in your power to uphold them
in their marriage?

All: We will.

The congregation remains standing. The husband and wife kneel and say together:

Heavenly Father,
we offer you our souls and bodies,
our thoughts and words and deeds,
our love for one another.
Unite our wills in your will,
that we may grow together
in love and peace
all the days of our life;
through Jesus Christ our Lord. Amen.

The minister will then bless the couple. There is also provision here for a sermon to be preached and a hymn to be sung.

Concluding prayers

The compilers of this service have been sensitive to the fact that many couples already have children from previous marriages, and/or together, and provide both a prayer 'For the gift of children', as in the marriage service, and two others, entitled 'For families', reprinted here:

> Father of all life,
> whose promise is to be the God of all the families of your
>   people,
> give grace to N and N in their new life together
> and bless those for whom they care.
> Enfold them in your love
> as they share in their new family,
> that they may grow up in all things into Christ,
> who gave himself that all humanity might be made one in
>   him. Amen.

> Heavenly Father,
> we are your children, made in your image.
> Hear our prayer
> that fathers and mothers, sons and daughters,
> may find together the perfect love that casts out fear,
> walk together in the way that leads to eternal life,
> and grow up together into the full humanity of your
>   Son Jesus Christ our Lord. Amen.

Prayers of penitence

It is recognized that many people who request a service of blessing have been divorced; although the Christian hope is that marriage is for life, it is acknowledged in most churches that life is not that simple and that we don't always manage to fulfil our resolves.

Some ministers have composed services to release divorced people from their vows, in order to enable them to put the past behind them and marry again. However, such 'services of release' are not recognized by the Anglican

Church. It maintains that vows made can never be reversed, but that we may acknowledge our failure, obtain God's forgiveness and move on. Where one or both partners feel the need for some kind of spoken repentance for past marital breakdown, such things can be arranged, maybe in a private service before the blessing service or even before the civil ceremony. This example by Clare Edwards from *Human Rites* could be adapted accordingly:

On the Occasion of a Second Marriage

Officiant: N, you have been married before and your marriage ended in divorce. Have you faced with honesty your part in the breakdown of that relationship?

Bride: I have.

Officiant: Have you allowed that experience to lead you into new life – to a better understanding of yourself and of your hopes and desires for the future?

Bride: I have.

Officiant: N, you have been married before and your marriage ended with your partner's death. Have you reflected on that relationship and faced with honesty your responsibility for both its weaknesses and its strengths?

Groom: I have.

Officiant: Have you allowed the experience of that marriage to lead you into new life – to a better understanding of yourself and of your hopes and desires for the future?

Groom: I have.

Officiant: Owning the past, are you, N, and you, N, each now ready to give yourself fully to the new marriage relationship which you believe God is offering you?

Both: I am.

The 'Services of Prayer and Dedication after Civil Marriage' do incorporate the general Prayers of Penitence for everybody present which are found in a normal service of Morning or Evening Prayer, and these may be considered sufficient. In saying these prayers, the whole congregation acknowledge that we all, at times, hurt our fellow men and women, either deliberately or accidentally, and ask and receive forgiveness. (See also 'Prayers for couples remarrying and for couples with children' in Chapter 6.)

Children taking part

If the couple have children of a suitable age, it would be highly appropriate to have them take part in some way, maybe to do one of the readings or recite a prayer of their own composition. They could enter and sit with their parents at the front of the church and stand with them during the dedication. A sensitive minister would involve and include them in the proceedings so that the whole family is blessed together, either as a new unit or as an existing one.

Other denominations

Other denominations are more likely to do their best to allow you to marry in their church, wherever possible. In other words, they would not bless a couple they couldn't or wouldn't marry: it would be considered an anomaly – one which the Church of England is currently working through. However, it is unlikely that any minister would refuse some kind of public blessing on a marriage, particularly if the couple had been married by civil ceremony some time ago but were now members of the church.

4

Vows and Promises

~~~~~⊷⊶⊷~~~~~

*A*ll couples in love make promises like 'I'll love you forever', often without thinking too hard about the implications of such a statement! The vows in the wedding service spell out the real meaning of marriage, as the couple, in effect, enter into a solemn contract with one another in public and before God. Whatever language or imagery you use, your vows and promises should be an expression of your earnest wish to be there for one another, whatever may happen in the future.

The Anglican marriage service

Since most people are familiar with the Anglican ASB marriage service, we will use it as our starting point, and then elaborate on it. The vows come immediately after the priest's welcome and introduction at the beginning of the service, and proceed as follows:

31

8. The priest says to the couple: The vows you are about to take are to be made in the name of God, who is judge of all and who knows all the secrets of our hearts: therefore if either of you knows a reason why you may not lawfully marry, you must declare it now.

9. Stand. The priest says to the bridegroom: N, will you take N to be your wife? Will you love her, comfort her, honour and protect her, and, forsaking all others, be faithful to her as long as you both shall live?

He answers: I will.

10. The priest says to the bride: N, will you take N to be your husband? Will you love him, comfort him, honour and protect him, and, forsaking all others, be faithful to him as long as you both shall live?

She answers: I will.

11. Either: A) The priest may receive the bride from the hands of her father. The bride and bridegroom face each other. The bridegroom takes the bride's hand in his and says:
I, N, take you, N,
to be my wife,
to have and to hold
from this day forward;
for better, for worse,
for richer, for poorer,
in sickness and in health,
to love and to cherish,
till death us do part,
according to God's holy law;
and this is my solemn vow.

They loose hands. The bride takes the bridegroom's right hand in hers and says:
I, N, take you, N,
to be my husband,
to have and to hold
from this day forward;
for better, for worse,
for richer, for poorer,
in sickness and in health,
to love and to cherish,
till death us do part,
according to God's holy law;
and this is my solemn vow.

They loose hands.

12. Or: B) The priest may receive the bride from the hands of her father. The bride and bridegroom face each other. The bridegroom takes the bride's right hand in his, and says:
I, N, take you, N,
to be my wife,
to have and to hold
from this day forward;
for better, for worse,
for richer, for poorer,
in sickness and in health,
to love, cherish, and worship,
till death us do part,
according to God's holy law;
and this is my solemn vow.

They loose hands. The bride takes the bridegroom's right hand in hers, and says:

I, N, take you, N,
to be my husband,
to have and to hold
from this day forward;
for better, for worse,
for richer, for poorer,
in sickness and in health,
to love, cherish, and obey,
till death us do part,
according to God's holy law;
and this is my solemn vow.

They loose hands.

13. *The priest receives the ring(s). (S)he says*: Heavenly
Father, by your blessing, let this ring be to N and N a symbol of unending love and faithfulness, to remind them of
the vow and covenant which they have made this day;
through Jesus Christ our Lord. Amen.

**14. *The bridegroom places the ring on the fourth finger of
the bride's left hand, and holding it there, says*:**
I give you this ring
as a sign of our marriage.
With my body I honour you,
all that I am I give to you,
and all that I have I share with you,
within the love of God,
Father, Son, and Holy Spirit.

**15. *If only one ring is used, before they loose hands the
bride says*:**
I receive this ring
as a sign of our marriage.
With my body I honour you,
all that I am I give to you,

and all that I have I share with you,
within the love of God,
Father, Son, and Holy Spirit.

*16. If rings are exchanged, they loose hands and the bride
places a ring on the fourth finger of the bridegroom's left
hand and, holding it there, says:*
I give you this ring
as a sign of our marriage.
With my body I honour you,
all that I am I give to you,   •
and all that I have I share with you,
within the love of God,
Father, Son, and Holy Spirit.

17. The priest addresses the people: In the presence of
God, and before this congregation, N and N have given
their consent and made their marriage vows to each
other. They have declared their marriage by the joining of
hands and by the giving and receiving of a ring. I therefore proclaim that they are husband and wife.

18. The priest joins their right hands together and says:
That which God has joined together let not man divide.

The only real choice laid down in the ASB service above is
whether the bride chooses to obey (and her groom to worship in return) or not, and whether the vows are symbolized
by one or two rings. In the BCP service there isn't provision
for the bride to give the groom a ring and promise to share
her worldly goods with him, though a priest would probably
consent to add this.

Actions speak louder than words

There is not much room for manoeuvre in the extract shown above, apart from the odd word the priest might allow. For example, 'respect' might be substituted for 'honour' in sections 14–16 or 'serve' added after 'to love and to cherish' in section 11. Remember, though, that actions are powerful and the way the vows are orchestrated within the service can make quite an impact. Some suggestions are outlined below.

The arrival of the bride and groom

Charles Read, in his booklet *Revising Weddings*, suggests that bride and groom could arrive at the church together; the priest would meet them both at the church door and the Introduction and sections 8–10 of 'The Marriage Service' would be conducted from there. The couple would then process to the front of the church for the rest of the service. This idea came out of the Roman Catholic Liturgical Conference of 1990 and has the effect of separating the legal requirements from the rest of the vows which are made before God. This would work in a church of any denomination if the minister were willing to comply.

How you decide to arrive in church is up to you. The traditional way is for the groom to arrive early and to wait at the front for the bride's entrance; she comes in escorted by her father or another male relative, with her attendants behind her. Bride and groom could just as well arrive together and walk down the aisle together. This would be appropriate if they already live together; they have already committed themselves to one another, so they come together to make their promises in public. If they have children, they could follow and stand just behind them at the front.

Placing of the vows

At many weddings, the actual marriage seems to happen all in a rush in the first few minutes almost before anybody realizes it, detracting from what is, after all, the most important part of the whole event. In the ASB there is an option for the readings and sermon to take place immediately after the opening sentence and prayer; this way the marriage takes place some 15 minutes further into the service. Your decision may depend on whether you think you'll be so nervous you want to get the vocal parts over as soon as possible, or whether you'd rather wait and give the vows more focus in the body of the service.

Being given away

Many women today find the idea of being handed over by one male to another, at best, quaintly archaic, or at worst, insulting, and therefore choose to arrive alone or with their attendants. I know of one older bride who just had a 'best woman' and they walked down the aisle together side by side. Even if the bride does choose to be escorted, it need not be by a man – why not her mother, godmother or another woman? She need not be 'given away' at all: that action is optional in the service.

Saying the vows

How you say the vows in section 11–16 is also up to you. Either you can repeat each phrase after the minister, or you could read the responses a section at a time from the prayer book or a printed sheet (make sure you remember your spectacles!), or you could learn them by heart. The latter is certainly impressive and very moving, particularly as bride and groom are facing one another at the time. But if you think your nerves might give out and cause you to dry up, or that you might get a fit of the giggles, don't risk it!

Writing your own vows

If you are marrying in any other than a Catholic or Anglican church, you will probably find you have far more room for creativity. Once the legal part is out the way, how you phrase your vows and what you add or subtract is largely up to you – with, of course, the approval of the person officiating. It is for you, as a couple, to decide what is important to you both. Although sections 11 and 12 of the ASB cover most eventualities in your future relationship, you may wish to be more explicit. For example:

> I, Ruth, take you, Tony,
> to be my husband,
> my one, true, life partner,
> for always in good times and when things get tough;
> in times of employment and prosperity
> and in times of unemployment and poverty;
> in times of health and times of sickness or despair,
> while we are young and when we are old;
> to love you, support you, respect you
> and encourage you for the rest of our lives,
> with God's help;
> and this is my promise to you today.

The above is also written in more normal, everyday language, though you may prefer to use the formality of the original. Another idea is to interweave your promises:

Tony: I take you, Ruth.
Ruth: I take you, Tony.
Tony: To be my wife.
Ruth: To be my husband.
Both: From this day forward and forever.
Tony: For better or for worse.
Ruth: In good times and when things get tough.
Tony: For richer and for poorer.
Ruth: In prosperity and in poverty.
Tony: In sickness and in health.
Ruth: While we are young and when we are old.
Tony: To love, encourage, and respect you.
Ruth: To love, support and cherish you.
Both: For the rest of our lives, with God's help, I promise.

Or you might like to use my version of the promises Ruth makes to her mother-in-law Naomi, in the Book of Ruth (Old Testament), chapter 1, verses 16 and 17:

Wherever you go, I will go;
And wherever you stay, I will stay;
Your people shall be my people,
And your God, my God.
Where you die, I will also die,
And there will I be buried with you.
May nothing but death part us
By God's help.

This might be appropriate if you envisage travelling for work in the future, or if you come from different religious or ethnic backgrounds, as did the two people in the story.

Additional promises together

If both partners are committed to a particular cause such as environmentalism, the peace and justice movement or some missionary enterprise, they might like to affirm that commitment together after their vows to one another. For example:

> *Both*: ... and together we promise to do our best to oppose injustice wherever it may be encountered.

Or:

> *Both*: ... and together we affirm our commitment to God's marvellous creation, to be good stewards and protect it against exploitation and destruction.

Including children in the vows

Some churches encourage the participation of any children of the couple being married and their inclusion in the vows and promises. The Wedding Service of the United Reformed Church includes the following:

> *In appropriate circumstances, the parents of A and C, and/or members of their families, and/or any children who will share in the new family, may be invited to stand and make the following promise*:
>
> Do you, __, give your blessing to this marriage of A and C, and promise always to support and encourage them?
>
> **We do**.

40

When there are children who will share in the new family the minister may say: A and C, will you be faithful, caring, and loving parents?

We will.

The congregation are also asked to express their support at this point. There seems to be no reason why such reciprocal promises of parents and children should not be inserted into the Anglican or any other denominational service. Ward and Wild's book *Human Rites* includes 'Celebrating the New Family: a ceremony for recognizing children during the wedding ceremony' by Dr Roger Coleman, to be inserted after the pronouncement of union between husband and wife:

Introduction

Officiant: Often marriage is viewed as the union of two individuals. In reality, however, marriage is much broader.

As we give thanks to God for the love which brings __ and __ together, so too we recognize the merging of families taking place and the additional love and responsibility family and friends bring to this relationship.

The unity of God's family

Officiant: We are, in fact, all members of one family, of God's family, a relationship emphasized in the Scriptures where it is written: 'And it was a happy day for God when we received our new lives, through the truth of God's word, and we became, as it were, the first children in God's new family' (adapted from James 1:18).

Recognition of children

Officiant: As part of the family nature of God's creation we recognize __ and the significant role he/she/they play(s) in this marriage today celebrated.

Child or children may be brought forward by grandparents or others if they are too young to stand as members of the wedding party.

Optional reading (for use when young children are involved)

Reader: The love and hope which God sends to us through the gift of each child finds expression in the Gospel of Mark: 'And they were bringing children to him, that Jesus might touch them; and the disciples rebuked them. But when Jesus saw it he was indignant, and said to them, "Let the children come to me, do not hinder them; for to such belongs the Kingdom of God." '

(An alternative reading is Psalm 127, substituting 'children' for 'sons'.)

Presentation of the family medallions [1]

Officiant: __ and __ present to __ this/these Family Medallion(s) created as a symbol for family unity and in recognition of the hope and joy made visible through this marriage.

1. The family medallion is a pendant depicting three equal circles, symbolizing the marriage union and the importance of the child within the new family; further details may be found at the end of this book. Alternatively, you could obtain something similar and have it engraved individually for each child.

The following may be repeated by the person performing the ceremony or one or both parents: In the placing of this/these medallions(s) we pledge to you, __, our continuing love even as we surround you now with our arms of support and protection.

Reading

Reader: Our children are gifts entrusted to us not as objects to be controlled but as separate in their own identity. Consider these words from *The Prophet* by Kahlil Gibran:

You may give them your love but not your thoughts,
For they have their own thoughts.
You may house their bodies but not their souls,
For their souls dwell in the house of tomorrow, which you
    cannot visit, not even in your dreams.
You may strive to be like them, but seek not to make them
    like you.
For life goes not backward nor tarries with yesterday.
You are the bows from which your children as living
    arrows are sent forth.

Prayer for the family

(Couple and children as well as congregation may be invited to hold hands.)

Officiant: Creator God, you have made us in your own image, male and female, that together we may live as members of your one family.

As you surround us with never-ending love, strengthen us that we, too, might reflect your love, becoming ever supportive of one another in times of sorrow, forgiving of one another in times of anger, patient in those moments when we seek to rebuild out of the pain of broken trusts and shattered dreams.

We give thanks, Lord, for the relationship here celebrated. In your presence we are humbled by the recognition that, today, we face a new future, one which love has unfolded and is unfolding before our very eyes.

May we ever respect the sanctity of this gift.

As you have filled our cup with joy, may we share the strength of our deepening love for one another, including, in ever widening circles, those who wait without hope and live without love's shelter. Amen.

Blessing

Officiant: 'For one person to love another – that is perhaps the hardest of all our tasks, the ultimate test and proof, the work for which all other work is but preparation . . . [Love] consists of this – that [we] protect and touch and greet each other.' (Rainer Maria Rilke, adapted.)

(Couple may kiss and then embrace children.)

Officiant: Go forth joined together by the love of God. Go forth with hope and joy and a heart full of dreams, knowing that God is always with you. Amen.

Introduction

Officiant: It is my pleasure to present to you __ and __ in their new relationship as husband and wife and their son/daughter/children __.

Or: Now I present to you the __ family.

If you feel the text above is too long or too wordy but the idea appeals, why not show it to the minister concerned and ask if they will help you can write something similar, appropriate to your own needs?

Congregational promises

All Christian marriage services include prayers for the couple (see Chapter 5), but in some churches the congregation present are asked to vocalize their support, as in the United Reformed Church service:

> *The congregation may then be invited to make the promise*: And do you, as friends of A and C, promise to support and encourage them in their marriage?

> **We do.**

Surprisingly, there is no such promise in the Anglican service, but why not ask for it to be inserted? Couples marrying today, with all the attendant pressures, might feel much encouraged to hear the spoken pledge of support and encouragement from their family and friends.

5

Symbols of Commitment

Rings

The giving of rings is an ancient custom and many people assume that this is what seals the vows and makes the marriage 'real'. In fact, the ring (or rings) is a symbol or picture of 'unending love and faithfulness' (ASB), 'a reminder of the promises made' (United Reformed Church Wedding Service) – and is a very potent symbol in our culture. Usually, a lot of thought goes into choosing wedding rings – after all, you hope to be wearing them for a very long time – and they may be an expression of your beliefs and values too.

Some people are concerned about exploitation in gold mining areas of the world and prefer to buy second-hand or use family rings; Welsh gold is rare and beautiful and does not (so far as we know!) involve exploitation of workers. When apartheid was still rife, the author and her husband chose rings which were guaranteed not to be mined under an oppressive regime. They have the Anti-Apartheid mark inside them and at the time were an expression of their beliefs, though nobody else knew their significance.

Rings don't, of course, need to be made of precious metal – no one can stop you using a couple of brass curtain rings;

it's been done before! You may even elect not to wear wedding rings afterwards, in which case the ones used in the service could be tiny circlets of flowers, or something similar. Rings are not the only symbol which can be used in the marriage service; some additions and alternatives gleaned from other cultures and traditions follow.

•

Coins

There is, apparently, an old Irish custom where the groom presents the bride with gold and silver. This could be adapted whereby the couple exchange gifts of jewellery (preferably something small like a neck chain or earrings) after the rings. Children could also be included here, using the Family Medallions mentioned in the previous chapter.

Candles

Candles may be used in a number of ways: to symbolize two becoming one; to give a picture of a bright new thing coming into existence; or as (de)light being shared among those present. Here are some ideas:

Catholic churches and some Anglican churches have a big Paschal candle at Easter which often remains in the church and may be lit for the service. The couple could each light a taper from the Paschal candle and together light a single candle of their own. Large church candles are readily available at commercial outlets and one could be garlanded or decorated to match the wedding flowers. This could be taken away afterwards to the couple's home and lit again for anniversaries.

A similar ritual could be enacted by representatives from the two families, symbolizing a new family unit being created from the two. Here is a candle ceremony from the United Baptist Church, USA:[1]

The two outer candles of a triple-stemmed candelabra are lit.

Minister: The two outside candles of the centre candelabra have been lit to represent your lives at this moment. They are two distinct lights, each capable of going their separate ways. To bring bliss and happiness to your home, there must be the merging of these two lights into one light.

From now on your thoughts shall be for each other rather than for your individual selves. Your plans shall be mutual, your joys and sorrows shall be shared alike.

As you each take a candle and together light the centre one, you will extinguish your own candle, thus letting the centre candle represent the union of your lives. As this one light cannot be divided, neither shall your lives be divided but a united testimony in a Christian home. You will pray together at the family altar, worship together in the house of God. That home is the happiest that looks with confidence towards reunion in heaven.

A Christmas wedding could really go overboard with candle-light! On the pronouncement of the couple's union small candles could be lit throughout the church (perhaps beginning at the end of a row by the ushers or bridesmaids, and then lit one from another down the pews), as sometimes done in a carol service.

The author's husband wanted fireworks at this point in the service but, sadly, it was deemed too dangerous!

1. From *The Wedding Ceremony*, Revd John W. Bartol.

Flowers

The placing of flower garlands round the necks of the marriage couple is common in some cultures and would be a lovely thing for the couple to do for one another, if practicable.

The exchange of a single flower or a posy of flowers could also be very charming, all the more so if these were the only flowers carried by the couple from the beginning. If your marriage or blessing service were to take place by a river or lake, flowers could be thrown into the water as a symbol of the journey you are about to make together.

Many brides still opt for a veil which is worn down until either she arrives at the front of the church or until after she is married, but why not crown both bride and groom with flowers after the exchanging of rings? It would rely upon both already being bare-headed and could be carried out either by the officiant or another member of the wedding party.

In the Orthodox tradition, metal crowns are held over the bride and groom's heads by attendants as a symbol of God's special grace.

Canopies and banners

The use of a canopy is not just associated with the Jewish tradition, though if one of the couple had Jewish roots it would be most fitting; it is also found in the Lutheran Church. Made of fabric and supported on four poles, a canopy can be embroidered or appliquéd, decorated with flowers, and held above the couple during the marriage. An innovative couple might have one made and present it to the church for use by other couples, or they might take it away and hang it on the wall at home, particularly if it were embroidered with a suitable verse of scripture such as 'His banner over us is love' (Song of Solomon 2:4) or 'Beloved, let us love one another, for love is of God' (1 John 4:7).

A number of churches are now decorated with banners, made of needlework or collage with scriptural verses on them; there may be a special wedding banner which could be hung at the front of the church. If it's not your thing, refuse politely, or offer to supply your own.

Anointing with oil

If you think of marriage as a vocation – a special task requiring a special blessing from God – then this may be for you. It is commonly used in some church traditions at baptism, confirmation and the ordination of clergy. It has connotations of healing, equipping, commissioning and affirming in the task about to be undertaken and the minister may be prepared to do this for you before or during the service.

Sharing bread and wine

The most common way of doing this is, of course, in the Mass or Communion Service where all share bread and wine together. But if this would not be appropriate you might like to share a loving-cup of wine and/or bread after the pronouncement; it is an ancient symbol of trust and peace between people. In the Jewish marriage service, a cup or glass of wine is used, with the following words:

> *The officiant says*: This cup of wine is symbolic of the cup of life. As you share the one cup of wine, you undertake to share all that the future may bring; all the sweetness life's cup may hold for you should be sweeter because you

drink together. And, as you break the cup, remember that whatever drops of bitterness life may contain, they should be less bitter because you share them.

As we recite the blessings over the wine, we pray that God will bestow fullness of joy upon you.

Blessed art thou, O Lord our God, Ruler of the Universe, who hast created all things for thy glory.

Blessed art thou, O Lord our God, Ruler of the Universe, Creator of Man.

Blessed art thou, O Lord our God, Ruler of the Universe, who hast fashioned us in thine own image and hast established marriage for the fulfilment and perpetuation of life in accordance with thy holy purpose.

Blessed art thou, O Lord our God, Ruler of the Universe, Creator of the fruit of the vine.

The couple then drink from the single glass of wine which is subsequently wrapped in a napkin and crushed underfoot.

Variations of this tradition are to be found in many countries and the example above could easily be adapted. Your minister may not relish shards of broken glass all over the place, but that is not strictly necessary! Indeed, you might like to have a goblet or glass specially made for you in ceramic or glass, with your names and the date engraved on it, to keep as a reminder of the vows you have made together.

In *A Service of Blessing* by Malcolm Johnson, the couple share wine, salt and bread as good, earthy symbolism of the life they will share together:

Both: Our hearts and our bodies call out to the living God. We shall journey in his presence as long as we live; we shall fulfil our promises to him in the presence of his people.

The wine

A: You and I drink from one cup to remember the joys and happiness we shall continue to share with God's blessing and presence.

B: Blessed are you, the Eternal, our God who creates the fruit of the vine.

They each drink from the cup.

The salt

B: We taste salt to remember the bitter and unhappy times we shall share together.

A: Blessed are you, the Eternal, our God who gives us strength for suffering.

They each taste the salt.

The bread

A: You and I eat this bread to remember our daily life together. May God hallow the ordinary things of life through his blessing.

B: Blessed are you, the Eternal, Our God, who brings forth bread from the earth.

They eat bread.

We do not recommend trying to incorporate all of the above in one service, as it would dilute the effect for the witnesses, as well as the significance for those getting married. But if you think it would be meaningful, choose perhaps one or two symbols which illustrate or emphasize for you both the bond you are making with one another. This may be especially apt for those coming from different ethnic backgrounds or religions – an opportunity to symbolize your union on more than one level.

6

Prayers and Blessings

Why do we pray?

Christians believe that we may communicate with God
through prayer, either individually (on our own, in private),
or corporately (with other people, publicly). We talk to God
about the things that are happening to us and ask for wisdom, guidance and protection; we pray for the welfare of
other people whom we care about; sometimes we simply
ask for things.

All church services include prayers and the wedding service is no exception. It is an appropriate place for clergy and
congregation to ask God to help the couple in their future
life together, to give them courage, wisdom and strength
and to enable them to keep their vows to one another. The
couple may also like to pray for themselves and each other,
that their commitment to one another may prove absolute
and durable for their whole lives together. Whether you are
regular churchgoers and used to praying or whether you are
not, it doesn't matter: the Bible says that so long as we have
faith 'the size of a grain of mustard-seed', that is sufficient.
So, don't get into a theological tangle about it – just pray,
and be assured that God is listening!

Prayers from the ASB

During the ASB marriage service the priest will pray for the couple (section 24 onwards) and there are a number of alternative and additional prayers printed in the service book from which you may choose. I suggest you read them together and decide which you would like to be prayed for you. For example, the prayer for the gift of children may not be appropriate: you may have decided not to have children, or may already have completed your family, or you may be unable to have children. However, if you do want children of your own, or are hopeful of adopting or fostering in the future, the following example (section 26) would be a good one to choose:

> Heavenly Father,
> maker of all things,
> you enable us to share in your work of creation.
> Bless this couple in the gift and care of children,
> that their home may be a place of love,
> security and truth,
> and their children grow up
> to know and love you in your Son
> Jesus Christ our Lord. Amen.

The alternative prayer (section 27) positively acknowledges that those without children have energy and love to spare for other people:

> Lord and Saviour Jesus Christ,
> who shared at Nazareth the life of an
> earthly home:
> reign in the home of these your servants
> as Lord and King;

give them grace to minister to others
as you have ministered to men [*or* us],
and grant that by deed and word
they may be witnesses of your
saving love
to those among whom they live;
for the sake of your holy name. Amen.

You can choose one or two prayers from the additional prayers that follow (sections 31–38) which seem most apt for you. For example, no. 33 prays that the couple may '... have joy in one another, as living temples of the Holy Spirit'; no. 34 prays that '... their life together witness to your love in this troubled world; may unity overcome division'. All are slightly different. The BCP service does not have quite so much choice.

At this point the congregation joins in with The Lord's Prayer which comes in two versions: the older one with the 'thees' and 'thous' which most people know from school, and the modern language alternative. If the majority of your guests are more likely to be familiar with the older version, even if you yourselves are used to the other, it makes sense to use it as they will feel more comfortable saying it.

Writing your own prayers

Why not ask a friend to write and read an appropriate prayer for you, which would be a lovely gift to keep? Alternatively, you could write one of your own to say together. The person marrying you may be willing to help you find the right words for what you want to say. Basically, decide what are your aspirations and hopes for this marriage, and ask God's help to achieve them. If you need ideas or guidelines, a selection of ready-made prayers follow from which you can choose, or upon which you can base your own.

Prayers to pray for the couple

The following prayers may be prayed aloud by the minister or someone else and the congregation joins in with the 'Amen' (meaning 'let it be so') at the end. Bear in mind that anything requiring a more complicated response will need to be printed on the service sheet. Some of the following contain general requests on behalf of the whole company present, as well as specifically for the couple. More often than not, such prayers turn out to apply not only to the people getting married, but to a number of folk in the congregation – 'Just what I needed to hear,' someone will often say as they leave – and turn out to have more benefits than you originally imagined!

Four prayers of approach to God[1]

> O God, you are the creator of all things; you made us, and
>   you sustain us; we depend on you.
> For the gift of life, we praise you. For being able to think
>   about its meaning and purpose, we thank you.
> In the world without, and in our lives within, there is
>   much that is confusing and contradictory. Many voices
>   counsel us; many forces pressure us; many things
>   tempt us.
> We need your light to lead us, and your hand to hold us,
>   and your love to complete us.
> In Jesus' name we ask your blessing now. **Amen.**

1. These four prayers are by Don Milne.

Almighty and eternal God, in you we live and move and have our being: you have so created us for yourself that our hearts are restless until they rest in you. Grant us now purity of heart and strength of purpose, so that no selfish passion may hinder us from knowing your will, and no weakness from doing it; and that in your light we may see our life clearly, and in your service find perfect freedom; through Jesus Christ our Lord, **Amen.**

O Father in heaven, bless these friends of ours who are about to give their vows of faithfulness to each other and to live together in the covenant bond of marriage. Let your love become their love, so that in their lives together they may be more concerned about the other than themselves. Above all, help each of us to be silent partners as we pray for them in the coming days, and be ready to assist them with good counsel and a helping hand. In the name of Jesus, their Lord and ours, we pray, **Amen.**

O God our Helper, source of infinite love, bless us with a sense of your indwelling presence as we worship here. Keep us sensitive to the wonder of things which fill our days and give meaning to life. Deepen in us the level of our loving, both for those near and dear to us, and for those, who, though strangers, need our concern, **Amen.**

For the wedding day

We thank you, Lord, for the dawning of this day and for your love which is new every morning. We pray for those who are to be married today and ask that you will give them great joy in the fulfilment of their love. And we ask you to bless their parents with a sense of your nearness, and a great consciousness of belonging to each other; and to all who are called to share their lives in marriage grant faithfulness to their promise, through Jesus Christ our Lord, Amen.[2]

For a newly-married couple

Eternal God, creator of us all, we praise you for all the ways in which your love enters our lives, and for all the joys that can come to men and woman through marriage. Today we especially pray for __ and __ as they begin their married life. With them we thank you for the love and care of their parents, which has guided them to maturity and prepared them for this commitment. Give them strength to keep the vows they have made, to be loyal and faithful to each other, and to support each other throughout their life, that they may bear each other's burdens and share each other's joys. Help them to be honest and patient with each other, [to be wise and loving parents] and to welcome both friends and strangers into their home. In all their future together, may they enjoy each other and grow through the love they share, until, at the end of this life, you receive us all into your eternal kingdom, through Jesus Christ our Redeemer. Amen.[3]

For an older couple

Lord God, gracious and loving giver of all good gifts, we thank you for the gift of love, demonstrated fully in your dear Son, our Lord and Saviour, Jesus Christ.

Thank you for your presence among us here today as we joyfully celebrate with __ and __ in their marriage.

2. From *More Prayers for Today's Church*, ed. Dick Williams, Kingsway 1984.
3. From *Prayers for the People*, ed. Michael Perry, Marshall Pickering, 1992.

We ask you to bless them as they make their life-long commitment to one another, embarking on a new and exciting phase in their lives in company with you.

We pray that you will help them as they adjust to this new relationship and altered circumstances; may their lives be combined together in loving compromise whilst remaining themselves, the people that we love.

May they have patience, good humour, honesty, compassion and understanding with one another; slow to criticize and swift to forgive.

May each encourage and nurture in the other the special gifts which you have given them, and as they grow together may they develop new ones which they may exercise both individually and together, for your glory.

May their home always be a place of peace and security, a place where you dwell as an honoured guest. May it be a place of hospitality and welcome for both friend and stranger, and a safe haven for their love.

In all things may they look to you for guidance and support throughout their lives.

Father, greatly bless our dear friends __ and __, that they may live a long, happy, healthy and fulfilling life together; and may we, as their friends and family, always be willing to support them and pray for them in whatever lies ahead. We place them now in your safe-keeping, Lord, knowing we can do no better.

All these things we ask in Jesus' name. **Amen.**[4]

O God, we pray for __ and __ who want to begin their life together with you and always continue it with you.

Help them never to hurt and never to grieve one another.

4. Rowena Edlin-White, for the marriage of Janet and Russell Kitson.

Help them to share all their work, all their hopes, and all their dreams, all their successes and all their failures, all their sorrows and all their joys. Help them to have no secrets from one another, so that they may truly be one.

Keep them always true to one another, and grant that the years ahead may draw them ever closer to one another. Grant that nothing may ever make them drift apart.

As they live with one another, help them to live with you, so that their love which they are to pledge now may grow perfect in your love, for you are the God whose name is love. This we ask in Jesus' name. **Amen.**

Gracious God, bless this man, __, and this woman, __, who come now to join themselves together in marriage, that they may give their vows to each other in the strength and spirit of your faithful love. Let the promise of your Word root and grow in their lives. Grant them vision and hope to persevere in trust and friendship all their days. Keep ever before them the needs of your world. By your grace enable them to be true disciples of Jesus Christ, in whose name we pray. **Amen.**

Out of this tangled world, O God, you have drawn __ and __ together and are binding them firmly by the sure insights of love. We thank you for the homes in which they have been nurtured in their formative years; for parents who have sacrificed in their behalf; for the Church which has awakened them to the meaning of eternal life.

Loving God, bless them as they come before you and their families and friends to affirm the choice that they have made of each other and their intention to establish a home where your love may be celebrated in the family. Grant them a seriousness of purpose that they may be kept from empty words and casual commitments. Be with them and let your love be the example and the power to help their love grow. May you nurture them all the days of their lives that their dreams and their aspirations for life may find fulfilment in the doing of your will in all things. We ask this in Jesus' name. **Amen.**[5]

Prayers for the couple to pray

Giving

O Divine Master, grant that
I may not so much seek
To be consoled as to console;
Not so much to be understood as to understand;
Not so much to be loved as to love;
For it is in giving that we receive;
It is in pardoning that we are pardoned;
It is in dying that we awaken to eternal life.

St Francis of Assisi

Belonging

Lord, we know that all our possessions are truly yours and, because our lives are in your hands, we have each other in trust from you. Grant us to regard each other as yours first of all, and so to honour and care for our partner as someone who belongs to God; someone whom we have been given to look after; in Jesus Christ our Lord. **Amen.**

For every day

'This is the day which the Lord had made; let us rejoice and be glad in it.'

Heavenly Father, help us to be aware of your presence each new morning; teach us your ways and let us respond to you with love and complete trust. Thank you for the

5. Three prayers above are by Don Milne.

precious gift of life: let us use each day to fulfil your divine purpose. Our times are in your hand: hold us fast for Jesus' sake. **Amen.**

For our future

God of new beginnings, we offer joyful thanks to you for the years ahead: help us to use them and not waste any part of them; may we live each day with Jesus as our friend and guide; teach us to value all that is good in the days to come, and help us to cope with any difficult times – we know you are with us in sunshine and shadow. Show us how to care and share, to give and forgive, and let the beauty of Christ touch us so that each day we may reflect his perfect love. This marriage is the start of our future – thank you for giving it to us: we commit ourselves to you, for the sake of your dear Son, Jesus Christ. **Amen.**[6]

God of tenderness and strength,
you have brought our paths together
and led us to this day;
go with us now as we travel through good times,
through trouble, or through change.
Bless our home, our partings and our meetings.
Make us worthy of each other's best,
and tender with each other's dreams,
trusting in your love in Jesus Christ.
Amen.[7]

6. Three prayers above from *Prayers for the People*, ed. Michael Perry, Marshall Pickering, 1992.
7. From 'The Marriage Service', *A New Zealand Prayer Book*, Collins Liturgical Publications, 1989.

Prayers by the bride and groom[8]

Groom: Eternal God, help me to be a loving husband to __.
Make firm in my life the vows of marriage that I may walk
in your will and be the person you would have me be.

Bride: Heavenly Father, guide me and help me to be the
person you would have me be, so that I may be a loving
wife to __ in the years ahead.

Both: O God, our Father, we kneel before you in the belief
that you have brought us together, helped our love to
grow and continue to be with us in a special way. We ask
you to stay by our side in the years ahead. Protect us from
anything which might harm this marriage, give us
courage when difficulties come our way, and teach us to
forgive one another when we fail.

Groom: I ask for the help I need to be a good husband and
father. Never let me take __ for granted, be unfaithful to
her, or fail to respect her. If we should be blessed with
children I promise to love them, provide for them, be
available for them, and give them the best possible
example.

Bride: I ask for the help I need to be a good wife and
mother. May I always love, encourage and be faithful to
__. If we should have children I promise to love them,
care for them, be available to them and, when the time
comes, to let them go.

Both: Finally we ask that in our old age, we may love one
another as deeply and cherish one another as much, and

8. Adapted from *A Marriage Service for You*, Robert J. Peterson, CSS
Publishing, 1977.

more, than we do at this moment. May our prayers
be granted through your Son, our Saviour Jesus Christ.
Amen.

Prayers for everyone to pray

Almighty God, our heavenly Father,
who gave marriage to be a source of
blessing to mankind [humankind],
we thank you for the joys of family life.
May we know your presence and peace
in our homes;
fill them with your love,
and use them for your glory;
through Jesus Christ our Lord. Amen.[9]

We commend to you, O Lord, our souls and bodies, our
minds and our thoughts, our prayers and our hopes, our
health and our work, our life and our death; our wives
and husbands, our parents and brothers and sisters, our
benefactors and friends, our neighbours, our fellow coun-
trymen and woman, and all Christian people, this day and
always. **Amen.**

Lancelot Andrewes (1555–1626)

I said to the man who stood at the Gate of the Year, 'Give
me a light that I may tread safely into the unknown.' And
he replied, 'Go out into the darkness and put your hand
into the hand of God. That shall be to you better than
light and safer than a known way.'

9. 'The Marriage Service', *Alternative Service Book* (1980), section 38.

May that Almighty hand guide and uphold us all;
through Jesus Christ our Lord. Amen.

Minnie Louise Haskins (1875–1957) *adapted*

A time to love ...
God,
you are the source of love
and you join us together in the miracle
of friendship, marriage and family life.
Let faithfulness, freshness and unselfishness
fill the deep relationships we cherish
and be a sign to the nations
that this is the way you love the world
in Jesus Christ our Lord.

... and a time to hate
God,
even with those who are closest and dearest
there are moments of anger and hurt.
Please have patience with us
when we destroy what is beautiful
through our failure to listen
and through our obsession with ourselves.
Amen.[10]

O Lord seek us, O Lord find us
In thy patient care,
Be thy love before, behind us,
Round us everywhere.
Lest the god of this world blind us,

10. From *Further Everyday Prayers*, David Jenkins, National Christian
    Education Council, 1992.

Lest he bait a snare,
Lest he forge a chain to bind us,
Lest he speak us fair,
Turn not from us, call to mind us,
Find, embrace us, hear.
Be thy love before, behind us,
Round us everywhere.

                              Christina Rossetti (1840–94)

Prayers for couples remarrying and for couples with children

For the remarried

God of mercy and new hope, we pray for all those who are remarried after the trauma of divorce, and for their partners. You read their hearts and minds; you know the inhibitions and the comparisons; you understand the readjustments they must continually make; you know the shadows of past failure and the weight of obligation to bygone unhappiness. In Christ you lift our burdens and sustain us: for such refreshment and strength we bring to you those whom you love; in Jesus' name. Amen.[11]

For forgiveness and healing

God of love and understanding, we know that it is impossible for people to live together without sometimes causing pain or misunderstanding. Help us to recognise our part in this failure and to know your forgiveness and healing of the past. In particular, we ask that your love may heal any hurtful memories that N and N may bring

11. From *Prayers for the People*, Michael Perry.

to this day. May they know your forgiveness and the peace that comes from your presence, now and always. **Amen.**[12]

For a parent's remarriage: as part of the marriage ceremony
During the marriage ceremony, the children join the couple at the time of the blessing. They kneel with the parents, and the priest says the following prayer:

> **Bless, O God, this new family especially (names of children). Surround them with love; give them a secure and stable home and a sense of belonging. Protect them from all danger, support them in times of trouble, and give them peace. Grant them knowledge that __ and __'s love for one another includes them in that love and that they are an essential part of this family; in the name of Jesus Christ we pray. Amen.**
>
> Vienna Cobb Anderson

Belonging (children)
> **God, our Father, we are taught that children are a blessing and a gift from you: give us that perfect balance of care and trust which you show towards us; strengthening us both to protect them and to release them. When we can no longer guide them as we would, take them into your arms; through Jesus Christ our Lord. Amen.**[13]

Prayers remembering those who can't be present

Weddings churn up all sorts of emotions, especially for those who have lost a partner, parent or child; it is quite usual to acknowledge this in a brief prayer.

12. From 'An experimental liturgy for the blessing of a relationship', Anglican Diocese of Christchurch, New Zealand.
13. From *Prayers for the People*, Michael Perry.

Hear us as we remember those who have died in the peace of Christ, both those who have confessed the faith and those whose faith is known to you alone, and grant us with them a share in your eternal kingdom. Lord, have mercy.

The Alternative Service Book

Commemoration

God of the living, and Father of our risen Lord, we are glad in your presence today as we remember those who have gone before us believing in your promises and trusting in your mercy. Help us to follow them, as they have followed Christ, and with all your people on earth and in heaven to give you the glory and the praise that is your due: through Jesus Christ our Lord. Amen.[14]

For the bereaved

We remember, Lord, the slenderness of the thread which separates life from death, and the suddenness with which it can be broken. Help us also to remember that on both sides of that divide we are surrounded by your love. Persuade our hearts that when our dear ones die neither we nor they are parted from you. In you may we find our peace, and in you be united with them in the glorious body of Christ, who has burst the bonds of death and is alive for evermore, our Saviour and theirs, for ever and ever. Amen.[15]

14. From *Prayers for the People*, Christopher Idle.
15. From *Prayers for Today's Church*, Dick Williams.

Blessings

Blessings are different to prayers; they are a consecration in the name of God, a 'setting apart' and a 'sending out'. Customarily, the couple will receive a blessing from the priest or minister immediately after their marriage which expresses the hope that God will grant happiness and prosperity to the relationship, and the sign of the cross will be made over them.

God the Father,
God the Son,
God the Holy Spirit,
bless, preserve, and keep you;
the Lord mercifully grant you the
riches of his grace,
that you may please him both in body and soul,
and, living together in faith and love,
may receive the blessings of eternal life. **Amen.**[16]

The Lord who remembers us all – humble and great alike – bless you that fear him; the Lord prosper your way, the Lord bless your children; the Lord, the maker of heaven and earth bless you both now and evermore. **Amen.**

From Psalm 115

The Lord bless you all the days of your life: may you have prosperity; may you live to see your children's children: and the love of God, the Father, Son and Holy Spirit enrich you always. **Amen.**

From Psalm 128[17]

16. *Alternative Service Book*, section 19.
17. Blessings based upon Psalms both from *Prayers for the People*, Michael Perry.

Four Celtic 'sainings' or blessings

May the God who goes before us bless to you all those whom you shall meet, and may those who touch your lives bestow on you a lasting goodness. May the God who sets us in the community bless to you the friends you count already true and dear, and the friends you shall yet make. May the God who places us within the bonds of family bless to you the people who have always loved you and who will love you always, and may God bless to you the family that you yourselves become.

May God bless to you __, this man, __, and may God bless to you __, this woman, __.

May the God of peace guard
the door of your house,
the door of your heart.
May the road rise to meet you,
and the sun stand at your shoulder.
May life itself befriend you
each day, each night,
each step of your journey.
Amen.

The peace of God be with you.
The peace of Christ be with you,
The peace of Spirit be with you
    And with your children,
From the day that we have here to-day
    To the day of the end of your lives,
    Until the day of the end of your lives.

The grace of God be with you,
   The grace of Christ be with you,
The grace of Spirit be with you
   And with your children,
For an hour, for ever, for eternity.[18]

Christ as a light illumine and guide you,
Christ as a shield o'ershadow you;
Christ under you,
Christ over you,
Christ beside you
On your left and your right,
This day and forever.
Amen.[19]

18. *Carmina Gadelica*, vol. III, pp. 209, 211.
19. Adapted from 'Canticle', *Celtic Daily Prayer*, ed. the Northumbria Community, Marshall Pickering, 1994.

7

Bible Readings

~~~❧❀☙~~~

Choosing your readings

*A*t least one passage of scripture must be read during the Anglican Marriage Service, either at the beginning of the service or after the actual marriage. If the marriage includes Holy Communion there will be two Bible readings of which one must be a Gospel reading (from Matthew, Mark, Luke or John). This requirement is pretty standard whichever church you are married in, unless it is a Quaker Meeting; the idea is that we have the opportunity to hear what God says about this particular human activity, either in general or specific terms. In addition, a non-biblical reading of a suitable nature may also be used – you may have a favourite poem or piece of prose which means a lot to you, or one of the pieces in Chapter 8 might appeal; discuss it with the Minister beforehand. It is your day and you should choose readings which speak to you, or which embody some truth which is important to you.

73

Who reads?

You can ask anyone you would like to read, although it would be wise to choose people who feel confident about reading in public. Bear in mind, for example, that young children are not usually a good choice, as they tend to gabble and are unable to project their voices so that everyone can hear (many churches these days have a PA system and/or a Hearing Loop for the hard of hearing, but don't bank on it!). Your readers could be close friends, a brother or sister, or even the best man or a bridesmaid. It has been known for the wedding couple to do their own readings but, frankly, it's just one more thing to worry about, so I don't recommend it. It's much more pleasant to be able to relax for a few moments and listen to your chosen passage read to you. Make sure whoever reads has a copy of the material well in advance so they can familiarize themselves with it and practise. It will probably be easier for them to read from a single sheet of paper on the day, rather than having to juggle a Bible along with everything else.

Which Bible?

Your minister will probably have a list of suggestions of popular wedding readings from which you can choose; or you may want to go for something completely different. What you might find confusing is the number of different versions or translations of the Bible in use: the Authorized Version (sometimes referred to as the 'King James'), Revised Standard Version, Good News, New English ... what is the difference? You could simply ask the vicar if you can borrow a copy of the version they use in this particular church, or you may have a favourite of your own. It is not customary at weddings for the congregation to follow the reading in the Bibles in the pews, so don't feel tied to that. The reader could announce which version it is taken from to avoid confusion.

The Authorized Version (sixteenth century) is the earliest version we have, but not many churches still use it regularly. However, it is wonderfully poetic language for reading a psalm, or the Song of Songs, for instance. The Revised Authorized and New Revised Standard versions retain an elegance of language whilst doing away with the 'thees and thous'; the New International Version (NIV) is very popular and is a modern language Bible, easy to understand; the Good News Bible is more simplified still, but widely used. There are others: your local library should have a selection you can browse through.

Colossians chapter 3, verses 12–17, is a very popular reading for a wedding; in it, St Paul tells one of the early churches how its members should love one another – but it applies just as well between husbands and wives. Here are three different versions of the same passage:

Authorized Version

12. Put on therefore, as the elect of God, holy and beloved, bowels of mercies, kindness, humbleness of mind, meekness, long-suffering;
13. Forbearing one another, and forgiving one another, if any man have a quarrel against any: even as Christ forgave you, so also do you.
14. And above all these things put on charity, which is the bond of perfectness.
15. And let the peace of God rule in your hearts, to the which also ye are called in one body; and be ye thankful.

16. Let the word of Christ dwell in you richly in all wisdom; teaching and admonishing one another in psalms and hymns and spiritual songs, singing with grace in your hearts to the Lord.

17. And whatsoever ye do in word or deed, do all in the name of the Lord Jesus, giving thanks to God and the Father by him.

We don't tend to talk about our attitudes being formed in our bowels these days! Also, charity means something different to us: 'love' is a better translation. Word meanings have changed over the last three hundred years and we need to take that into account if the readings are going to mean something rather than sounding merely quaint.

New Revised Standard Version

As God's chosen ones, holy and beloved, clothe yourselves with compassion, kindness, humility, meekness and patience. Bear with one another and, if anyone has a complaint against another, forgive each other; just as the Lord has forgiven you, so you also must forgive. Above all, clothe yourselves with love, which binds everything together in perfect harmony. And let the peace of Christ rule in your hearts, to which indeed you were called in one body. And be thankful. Let the word of Christ dwell in you richly; teach and admonish one another in all wisdom; and with gratitude in your hearts sing psalms, hymns and spiritual songs to God. And whatever you do, in word or deed, do everything in the name of the Lord Jesus, giving thanks to God the Father through him.

This twentieth-century version is much more easily understood, speaking of love, forgiveness and harmonious living in 'the body' of the Church but also in the shared relationship of the married couple.

Good News Bible

You are the people of God; he loved you and chose you for his own. So then, you must clothe yourselves with compassion, kindness, humility, gentleness and patience. Be tolerant with one another and forgive one another just as the Lord has forgiven you. And to all these qualities add love, which binds all things together in perfect unity. The peace that Christ gives is to guide you in all the decisions you make; for it is to this peace that God has called you together in the one body. And be thankful. Christ's message in all its richness must live in your hearts. Teach and instruct each other with all wisdom. Sing psalms, hymns and sacred songs; sing to God with thanksgiving in your hearts. Everything you do or say, then, should be done in the name of the Lord Jesus, as you give thanks through him to God the Father.

The meaning of the passage is made very plain in this version.

Readings for your Wedding, edited by Brian Magee CM, is a resource aimed at people getting married in a Roman Catholic church but is perfectly applicable to any wedding; he shows passages in both the Jerusalem Bible and New Revised Standard Version translations, and includes readings from the Apocrypha (books not normally included in Bibles used by the Anglican and Nonconformist churches). He also gives useful hints and tips to help the reader.

Some popular Bible readings for weddings and blessings

We do not intend to reproduce every reading, but suggest you get hold of a Bible in a traditional or modern translation, whichever appeals, and look up some of the following.

Old Testament

Genesis 1:26–31
The story of the creation; God makes human beings, both male and female, in his own image and places them within the world, with responsibility for it.

Genesis 2:18–24
The 'other' Genesis story where God makes a partner for the man who then cries out ecstatically, 'At last! Bone of my bone and flesh of my flesh!' (author's version) emphasizing the oneness and compatibility of men and women.

Ecclesiastes 3:1–15
'A time to be born and a time to die': a particularly lovely passage made into a popular song in the sixties, about there being a time and a place for 'every activity under heaven'. It acknowledges pain and weeping as well as laughter and joy.

Ecclesiastes 4:9–12
'Two are better than one,' says this reading, and 'A cord of three strands is not easily broken'. In other words, the marriage which includes God remains strong.

Psalm 23
'The Lord is my Shepherd': a well-known favourite, either spoken or sung.

Psalm 103
Praising God for his care for us, his justice, compassion and faithfulness 'from everlasting to everlasting'. This is quite a long psalm; two people could share it, speaking alternate verses.

Psalm 104
A tremendous hymn of praise to God who has created a wonderful world intended to live in harmony and co-operation – ideal for environmentalists! Again, this is rather long, so could be edited somewhat.

Psalm 139:1–18, 23–24
A lovely psalm describing how God already knows everything about us so there is no need to pretend: 'You have searched me and you know me,' the psalmist says, 'you knit me together in my mother's womb ... I am fearfully and wonderfully made.'

Song of Songs 3:1–11
Sometimes called the 'Song of Solomon', a poetic celebration of physical love, of truly sensuous beauty. This passage describes the beloved one searching for her lover: 'I search for the one my heart loves ...'; it is full of exotic imagery and is richest in the old Authorized Version.

Song of Songs 6:3; 7:10; 8:6–7, 14
I am my beloved's, and my beloved is mine. I am my beloved's and his desire is towards me.

Set me as a seal upon thine heart, as a seal upon thine arm: for love is strong as death; jealousy is cruel as the grave: the coals thereof are coals of fire, which hath a most vehement flame. Many waters cannot quench love, neither can the floods drown it: if a man would give all the substance of his house for love, it would utterly be condemned. Make haste, my beloved, and be thou like a roe or to a young hart upon the mountains of spices. (A compilation from the Authorized Version.)

Ruth 1:1–17

A story about loyalty and love. Ruth insists upon staying with her mother-in-law, even in a foreign country; it contains the promise: 'Wherever you go, I will go ... your people shall be my people.'

Ruth 3:1–18; 4:13–17

The love story of Ruth and Boaz – in which Ruth takes the initiative!

Proverbs 3:3–12

Trust God, '... and he will make your paths straight.'

Proverbs 14:26–27; 15:33; 16:6; 22:4; 29:25

The following is a compilation of pithy sayings from the Proverbs of Solomon, New International Version. Actually, you could pick out several of these sayings yourself and put them together in a reading – be warned, they are often contradictory!

He who fears the Lord has a secure fortress,
and for his children it will be a refuge.
The fear of the Lord is a fountain of life,
turning a man from the snares of death.

The fear of the Lord teaches a man wisdom,
and humility cometh before honour.

Through love and faithfulness sin is atoned for;
through the fear of the Lord a man avoids evil.

Humility and fear of the Lord
bring wealth and honour and life.

Fear of man will prove to be a snare,
but whoever trusts in the Lord is kept safe.

Proverbs 31:10–31
'The wife of good character' who is worth more than rubies;
she is an astute business woman and a good mother, charitable and wise – this should appeal to today's woman, but is
a lot to live up to!

Revelation 19:6–9
The glorious vision of the wedding feast of the Lamb (Jesus)
and his bride, the Church.

New Testament: Gospel readings

Matthew 5:1–12
This passage is sometimes known as the Beatitudes. Jesus
repeats the phrase, 'Blessed are ...' and goes on to tell us – to
our surprise – that it is not necessarily the wealthy, the suc-
cessful and the powerful who are blessed by God, but rather
the weak, the marginalized and the sorrowful. 'Blessed are
the peacemakers, for they shall be called the children of
God.' A suitable passage for all couples engaged with social
justice.

Matthew 22:1–14
Jesus tells a parable (a story with a double meaning) about
a wedding; a lot of people are invited but many have excuses
why they can't come. So the host brings in strangers and
passers-by instead. The feast Jesus refers to is the kingdom
of heaven, but in modern terms this might be apposite

where there is social or family opposition to a marriage; it might say to you, 'Don't worry, there are plenty of other people willing to celebrate with you.'

Mark 10:6–16
The teachings of Jesus about marriage (the two become one in their commitment to one another), and about the special place of children.

John 2:1–11
The story of Jesus turning the water into wine at the wedding in Cana which is mentioned in the Introductions of the BCP and ASB wedding services. It's OK to let your hair down – Jesus enjoyed a good party too! Also, these readings are a reminder that Jesus turns the ordinary and commonplace into something special.

John 15:9–17
A famous passage about the nature of true love: generous, unselfish and affecting those around you. It speaks to the whole assembly, not just the wedding couple.

New Testament: other

1 Corinthians 13:1–13 (or just 1–7)
Speaks of love as the greatest gift, more important than anything else: 'Love never fails ... bears all things, believes all things, hopes all things, endures all things.' Something to aspire to.

Ephesians 3:14–21
A prayer by St Paul, that everyone may know the love of Christ 'which passes all understanding'.

Ephesians 5:22–33

This is the infamous passage about wives submitting to their husbands. The concept of submission has altered over the years to suggest one person being dominated by another, yet many people still choose this reading. If you do, I recommend the New Jerusalem or New Revised Standard versions included in 'Readings for your Wedding' as being much more acceptable and accurate translations, in which both partners submit lovingly to one another.

Colossians 3:12–17

Patience, long-suffering and forgiveness – printed in full in the three versions shown above.

Philippians 2:1–11

St Paul is speaking to the church at Philippi, urging them to act with humility towards one another, not to be selfish or conceited, 'having the same love, being in one spirit and purpose'. Can just as readily be applied to the family situation.

1 John 4:7–21 (or just 7–12)

'Beloved, let us love one another, for love is of God ...' God's love is proven to us through his gift of Jesus. 'Perfect love casts out fear' is another famous line from this passage, which may speak personally to couples who feel apprehensive about the future.

Old and New Testament mixed

Blessed is the one who trusts in the Lord, whose confidence is in him. He will be like a tree planted by the water that sends out its roots by the stream. It does not fear when heat comes; its leaves are always green. It has no worries in a year of drought and never fails to bear fruit.

So then, just as you received Christ Jesus as Lord, continue to live in him, rooted and built up in him, strengthened in the faith as you were taught, and overflowing with thankfulness.

Grow in the grace and knowledge of our Lord and Saviour Jesus Christ.

To each one of us grace has been given as Christ apportioned it ... to prepare God's people for works of service, so that the body of Christ may be built up until we all reach unity in the faith and in the knowledge of the Son of God and become mature, attaining to the whole measure of the fullness of Christ. Then we will no longer be infants, tossed back and forth by the waves, and blown here and there by every wind and teaching and by the cunning and craftiness of men in their deceitful scheming. Instead, speaking the truth in love, we will in all things grow up into him who is the head, that is, Christ.

(Compilation of Jeremiah 17:7–8, Colossians 2:6–7, 2 Peter 3:18, Ephesians 4:7, 12–15 in the New International Version.)

This compilation works because all the writers are addressing the same theme, but I wouldn't recommend splicing bits of scripture from different books yourself as the original contexts and meanings may be lost and it will cease to be a proper Bible reading.

Apocrypha

Tobit 8:4–8

On the evening of their marriage, Tobias said to Sarah, 'Let us pray and implore our Lord that he grant us mercy and safety.' Tobias began by saying,

'Blessed are you, O God of our ancestors,
and blessed is your name in all generations forever.
Let the heavens and the whole creation bless you forever.
You made Adam, and for him you made his wife Eve
as a helper and support.
From the two of them the human race has sprung.
You said, "It is not good that man should be alone;
let us make a helper for him like himself."
I now am taking this kinswoman of mine,
not because of lust,
but with sincerity.
Grant that she and I may find mercy
and that we may grow old together.'

And they both said, 'Amen, Amen.'

(New Revised Standard Version)

8

Additional Prose and Poetry Readings

~~~✦~~~

*H*ere are some suggestions for non-biblical readings which might be used during the marriage service, or for private inspiration. They are divided into headings for easy reference. Those suitable for inclusion in a Civil Marriage Service (that is, they have no religious content or reference) are marked with an asterisk (*).

God is Love

Sing a New Song: *St Augustine of Hippo (d. 431 AD)*

In this reading, Augustine is saying that the love we find in one another has its origins in God, to whom we need to turn for constant renewal of our love; and that we should let God's love be reflected in our lives.

'Sing to the Lord a new song; his praise is in the assembly of the saints.' We are urged to sing a new song to the Lord, as singers who have learned a new song. A song is a thing of joy; more profoundly, it is a thing of love. Anyone, therefore, who has learned to love the new life has learned to sing a new song, and the new song reminds us of our new life. The new singer, the new song, the new covenant, all belong to the one kingdom of God, and so the new singer will sing a new song and will belong to the new covenant.

We cannot love unless someone has loved us first. The source of our love for God can only be found in the fact that God loved us first. This love is not something we generate ourselves; it comes to us through the Holy Spirit who has been given to us.

Now it is your unquestioned desire to sing of him whom you love, but you ask me how to sing his praises. You have heard the words: 'Sing to the Lord a new song', and you wish to know what praises to sing. The answer is: 'His praise is in the assembly of the saints'; it is in the singers themselves. If you desire to praise him, then live what you express. Live good lives, and you yourselves will be his praise.

From Revelations of Divine Love: *Mother Julian of Norwich (1342–1413)*

Julian was a visionary who saw all of life represented by a tiny object in the hand of God – unable to exist without God's sustaining love. Human love is part of the process by which God constantly re-creates the world.

Our Lord showed me a little thing, the size of a hazelnut, in the palm of my hand; and it was as round as a ball. I looked thereupon with the eye of my understanding, and thought, 'What may this be?' And it was generally answered thus, 'It is all that is made.' I marvelled how it might last, for I thought it might suddenly have fallen to nothing for littleness. And I was answered in my understanding, 'It lasts, and ever shall last, because God loves it. And so all things have their being by the love of God.'

And from that time it was showed, I desired often to know what was our Lord's meaning. 'Would you understand your Lord's meaning? Understand it well: Love was God's meaning. Who showed it to you? Love. What did he show you? Love. Why did God show it to you? For love.' Thus did I learn that Love was our Lord's meaning.

And I saw full surely in this and in all, that ere God made us God loved us; which love was never slackened nor ever shall be. And in this love God has done all that God made; and in this love God has made all things profitable to us; and in this love our life is everlasting. In our making we had beginning; for the love wherein God made us was in God from without beginning. And all this shall we see in God, without end. Which may Jesus grant us.

From The Hymn of the Universe:
Pierre Teilhard de Chardin (1881–1955) *

Teilhard de Chardin was a Jesuit palaeontologist who believed that the whole creation revolves around an 'Omega point' in which all will be united in love; the love you feel for each other is part of the universal purpose.

Only love can bring individual beings to their perfect completion, as individuals, by uniting them one with another, because only love takes possession of them and unites them by what lies deepest within them. This is simply a fact of our everyday experience. For indeed at what moment do lovers come into the most complete possession of themselves if not when they say that they are lost in one another? And is not love all the time achieving – in couples, in teams, all around us – the magical and reputedly contradictory feat of personalizing through totalizing? And why should not what is thus daily achieved on a small scale be repeated one day on world-wide dimensions?

Humanity, the spirit of the earth, the synthesis of individuals and peoples, the paradoxical conciliation of the element with the whole, of the one with the many: all these are regarded as utopian fantasies, yet they are biologically necessary; and if we would see them made flesh in the world what more need we do than imagine our power to love growing and broadening till it can embrace the totality of human beings and of the earth?

From Waiting on God: *Simone Weil (d.1943)*

Being in love makes us aware as never before of nearness and separation; love unites us across any distance, yet leaves us wanting to be closer and more deeply united. This, Weil says, is the mystery of God. A Frenchwoman of Jewish ancestry, Weil starved herself and died in solidarity with her compatriots during World War II.

Before all things, God is love. Before all things, God loves himself. This love, this friendship of God, is the Trinity. Between the terms united by this relation of divine love there is more than nearness; there is infinite nearness or identity. But, resulting from the Creation, the Incarnation and the Passion, there is also infinite distance. The totality of space and the totality of time, interposing their immensity, put an infinite distance between God and God.

Lovers or friends desire two things. The one is to love each other so much that they enter into each other and only make one being. The other is to love each other so much that, having half the globe between them, their union will not be diminished in the slightest degree. All any human being desires here below is perfectly realized in God. We have all these impossible desires within us as a mark of our destination.

The love between God and God, which in itself is God, is this bond of double virtue; the bond which unites two beings so closely that they are no longer distinguishable and really form a single unity, and the bond which stretches across distance and triumphs over infinite separation.

It is only necessary to know that love is a direction and not a state of the soul.

Love is ...

*'Love and Friendship': Emily Brontë (1818–48)**

This poem reminds us that love, and particularly a marriage relationship, needs friendship in order to develop and last.

> Love is like the wild rose-briar,
> Friendship like the holly-tree –
> The holly is dark when the rose-briar blooms
> But which will bloom most constantly?
>
> The wild rose-briar is sweet in spring,
> Its summer blossoms scent the air;
> Yet wait till winter comes again
> And who will call the wild-briar fair?
>
> Then scorn the silly rose-wreath now
> And deck thee with the holly's sheen
> That when December blights thy brow
> He may still leave thy garland green.

Sonnet 116: William Shakespeare (1564–1616)*

True love endures through thick and thin, it is much more
than 'skin-deep'.

Let me not to the marriage of true minds
Admit impediments. Love is not love
Which alters when it alteration finds,
Or bends with the remover to remove:
O, no! it is an ever-fixèd mark,
That looks on tempests and is not shaken;
It is the star to every wandering bark,
Whose worth's unknown, although his height be taken.
Love's not Time's fool, though rosy lips and cheeks
Within his bending sickle's compass come;
Love alters not with his brief hours and weeks,
But bears it out even to the edge of doom,
    If this be error, and upon me proved,
    I never writ, nor no man ever loved.

'Love Me Little, Love Me Long', Anonymous (sixteenth century)

Love me little, love me long,
Is the burden of my song:
Love that is too hot and strong
    Burneth soon to waste.
Still I would not have thee cold,
Not too backward nor too bold;
Love that lasteth till 'tis old
    Fadeth not in haste.
Love me little, love me long
Is the burden of my song.

'A definition of love': Donald A. Green (1949–82)*

Love is the will to nurture life and growth in oneself and in another ...

Love is personal, it is the sacred trust of living things; likewise, love is neither need nor dependency. 'I need you' is not the same as 'I love you'. Need as a basis of a relationship may lead one person to suffocate another through demands. Need may drive me to manipulate, intimidate, or coerce you into fulfilling me.

Love is so vastly different! It is freeing; it acknowledges the separateness of the beloved that is each one's contribution to the relationship. Love calls for submission and sacrifice. It does not seek to possess, but rather to empty itself in nurture of the loved one.

'Love Lies beyond the Tomb': John Clare (1793–1864)

Clare was one of the greatest English rural poets; this poem describes love as something which, even on earth, seems to link us with heaven.

Love lies beyond
The tomb, the earth, which fades like dew!
  I love the fond,
The faithful, and the true.

Love lies in sleep,
The happiness of healthy dreams:
  Eve's dews may weep,
But love delightful seems.

'Tis seen in flowers,
And in the even's pearly dew;
    On earth's green hours,
And in the heaven's eternal blue.

    'Tis heard in spring
When light and sunbeams, warm and kind,
    On angel's wing
Bring love and music to the mind.

    And where is voice,
So young, so beautifully sweet
    As nature's choice,
When spring and lovers meet?

    Love lies beyond
The tomb, the earth, the flowers, and dew.
    I love the fond,
The faithful, young, and true.

The marriage of true minds

From 'A Marriage Sermon': John Donne (c.1571–1631)

Every marriage is a part of God's purpose which began with
the Creation and will end with the kingdom of heaven. Your
marriage is part of the plan by which God is preparing us
for eternal life.

The first marriage that was made, God made, and he
made it in Paradise. The last marriage which shall be
made, God shall make too, and in Paradise too; in the
Kingdom of heaven: and at that marriage, I hope in him
that shall make it, to meet, not some, but all this
company. From all eternity in the Book of Life, in God's

eternal Decree for my election, there Christ was married to my soul. Before my soul was a soul, did Christ marry my soul in his eternal Decree. So it was eternal, it had no beginning. Neither doth he interrupt this by giving me any occasion of jealousy by the way, but loves my soul as though there were no other soul, and would have done and suffered all that he did for me alone, if there had been no name but mine in the Book of Life. And he hath married me to him, *in aeturnam*, for ever, before all beginnings, and *in aeturnam*, for ever, without any interruptions, so I know that *whom he loves he loves to the end*, and that he hath given me, not a presumptuous impossibility, but a modest infallibility that no sin of mine shall divorce or separate me from him. There where the Angels, which cannot die could not live, this very body which cannot choose but die, shall live, and live as long as that God of life that made it.

'Marriage is one long conversation': Robert Louis Stevenson (1850–94)*

Marriage is one long conversation, chequered by disputes. The disputes are valueless; they but ingrain the difference; the heroic heart of woman prompting her at once to nail her colours to the mast. But in the intervals, almost unconsciously, and with no desire to shine, the whole material of life is turned over and over, ideas are struck out and shared, the two persons more and more adapt their notions one to suit the other, and in process of time, without sound of trumpet, they conduct each other into new worlds of thought.

From The Irrational Season: *Madeleine L'Engle (contemporary)* *

Ultimately there comes a time when a decision must be made. Ultimately two people who love each other must ask themselves how much they hope for as their love grows and deepens, and how much risk they are willing to take. It is indeed a fearful gamble. Because it is the nature of love to create, a marriage itself is something which has to be created.

To marry is the biggest risk in human relations that a person can take. If we commit ourselves to one person for life this is not, as many people think, a rejection of freedom; rather it demands the courage to move into all the risks of freedom and the risk of love which is permanent; into that love which is not possession but participation. It takes a lifetime to learn another person.

When love is not possession, but participation, then it is part of that co-creation which is our human calling.

From The Prophet: *Kahlil Gibran (contemporary)*

The Prophet reminds the couple that, though joined, they are still individuals and must remain the separate selves that have drawn them to one another in the first place; they continue their journey together side by side, but not glued together.

Then Almitra spoke again and said, And what of Marriage, master?
And he answered saying:
You were born together, and together you shall be for evermore.
You shall be together when the white wings of death scatter your days.

Aye, you shall be together even in the silent memory of
God.
But let there be spaces in your togetherness.
And let the winds of the heavens dance between you.

Love one another, but make not a bond of love:
Let it rather be a moving sea between the shores of your
souls.
Fill each other's cup but drink not from one cup.
Give one another of your bread but eat not from the same
loaf.
Sing and dance together and be joyous, but let each one
of you be alone.
Even as the strings of a lute are alone though they quiver
with the same music.

Give your hearts, but not into each other's keeping.
For only the hand of Life can contain your hearts.
And stand together yet not too near together:
For the pillars of the temple stand apart,
And the oak tree and the cypress grow not in each other's
shadow.

'Bridal Day': Compton Mackenzie (1883–1972)*

This bridal day with gold I will enchain,
And wear its hours like rubies on my heart,
That you and I from Love may never part
While still these jewelled monuments remain.
These monuments, wrought out of hours, contain
The wound inflicted on me by Love's dart,
That stung with such intolerable smart,
Until to-day we vanquished Time and Pain.

And now I wear this crimson diadem
Where late my heart did incarnadine
With open wounds in passionate array,
Unhealed until your eyes looked down at them,
And crystallized their sanguine drops to shine
In captured moments of our bridal day.

'Wedding Day': Rowena Edlin-White*

Now comes the knitting, the tying, entwining into one,
Mysterious involvement of two, whole, separate people
Into something altogether strange and changing, new and
    lovely.
Nothing can ever be, we will never be, the same again:
Not merged into each other irrevocably, but rather
From now on we go the same way, in the same direction,
Agreeing not to leave each other lonely, or discouraged, or
    behind.
I will do my best to keep my promises to treasure you and
    keep you warm;
And we will make our wide bed beneath the bright
And ragged quilt of all the yesterdays that make us who
    we are,
The strengths and frailties we each bring to this marriage,
And we will be rich indeed.

'Never marry but for love': William Penn (1644–1718)

Never marry but for love; but see that thou lovest what is
lovely. He that minds a body and not a soul has not the
better part of that relation, and will consequently lack the
noblest comfort of a married life.

Between a man and his wife nothing ought to rule but love ... As love ought to bring them together, so it is the best way to keep them well together.

A husband and wife that love one another show their children (and servants) that they should do so too. Others visibly lose their authority in their families by their contempt of one another; and teach their children to be unnatural by their own examples.

Let not enjoyment lessen, but augment, affection; it being the basest of passions to like when we have not, what we slight when we possess.

Here it is we ought to search out our pleasure, where the field is large and full of variety, and of an enduring nature; sickness, poverty or disgrace being not able to shake it because it is not under the moving influences of worldly contingencies.

Nothing can be more entire and without reserve; nothing more zealous, affectionate and sincere; nothing more contented and constant than such a couple, nor greater temporal felicity than to be one of them.

'Marriage Song': George MacDonald (1824–1905)

'They have no more of wine!' she said.
But they had enough of bread;
And the vessels by the door
Held for thirst a plenteous store:
Yes, enough; but Love divine
Turned the water into wine!

When should wine like water flow,
But when home two glad hearts go!
When, in sacred bondage bound,
Soul in soul hath freedom found!

Such the time when, holy sign,
Jesus turned the water into wine.

Good is all the feasting then;
Good the merry words of men;
Good the laughter and the smiles;
Good the wine that grief beguiles;–
Crowning good, the Word divine
Turning water into wine.

Friends, the Master with you dwell!
Daily work this miracle!
When fair things too common grow,
Bring again their heavenly show!
Ever at your table dine,
Turning water into wine!

So at last you shall descry
All the patterns of the sky:
Earth a heaven of short abode;
Houses temples unto God;
Water-pots, to vision fine,
Brimming full of heavenly wine.

Till death us do part

*'Married Love': Kuan Tao-Sheng (thirteenth century)**

You and I
Have so much love,
That it
Burns like fire,
In which we bake a lump of clay
Molded into a figure of you
And a figure of me.

Then we take both of them,
And break them into pieces,
And mix the pieces with water,
And mold again a figure of you,
And a figure of me.
I am in your clay.
You are in my clay.
In life we share a single quilt,
In death we will share one coffin.

'The Birthday': Morley Jamieson (contemporary)

When we are at last in that far heaven
Where there is no more taking and giving
In marriage,
And we are pure beyond all error
Freed of delights, of joy or terror,
Without dear hands and feet,
And all that lies between, refined
Out of all knowledge –
That will be a late limbo.
But at the Day
The great mystery will open clear
And our bodies resurrect appear
Whole and without blemish;
The Fire that transmogrified the mind
Will make us what we
Always were, before mortality.
Then may we face eternity, with equanimity.
Beforehand, in those long spaces of God's art,
I can see our earthly shapes, our bones inert
Carved perpetually with desire, and linked
In loving and anguished image
Of the unending joy to come –

100

The unspoken word, the patient poise
Makes a past world of deepest sense,
A life, a time, that now is making,
Let us create with honest loving.

'Marriage and Death': E. J. Scovell (contemporary)

The poet seems to refer to the expression 'to die to self'
which is a prerequisite for marriage; having done this so
completely she contemplates physical death as a small step.

We are not dovetailed but opened to each other
So that our edges blur, and to and fro
A little wind-borne trade plies, filtering over,
Bartering our atoms when fair breezes blow.

Though, not like waters met and inter-running,
Our peoples dwell each under a different sky,
Here at high, unsurveyed, dissolving frontiers
We cannot prove: 'This is you, this is I.'

Oh now in you, no more in myself only
And God, I partly live, and seem to have died,
So given up, entered and entering wholly
(To cross the threshold is to be inside),

And wonder if at last, each through each far dispersed,
We shall die easily who loved this dying first.

The bride speaks of her husband

'A Sweet Thing is Marriage': Catherine de Pisan (1364–1431) trans. Helen R. Lane

A sweet thing is marriage
My example proves 'tis so
To anyone whose husband is
As wise and good as he
Whom God made me find.
Praised be He who would save me,
For he has sustained me every single day
Ah, indeed, the sweet man is fond of me ...

The first night of our marriage
He showed me forthwith how good a man he was
For he did attempt no violence
That might hurt me.
And before time to arise
He kissed me a hundred times, I remember
Without a single villainy
Ah, indeed, the sweet man is fond of me ...

He spoke these tender words to me:
"Tis God has brought me to you
Tender friend, for your sweet use
Methinks He wished to raise me up.'
He did not cease this reverie
The whole night through
Not once behaving in any other way
Ah, indeed, the sweet man is fond of me.

'Sonnet 43': Elizabeth Barrett Browning (1806–61)

When she was 40 the poet eloped against the wishes of her father. This jubilant declaration of love for her husband ends with an optimistic look forward to an eternity where human, earthly love will continue, strengthened by God.

How do I love thee? Let me count the ways.
I love thee to the depth and breadth and height
My soul can reach, when feeling out of sight
For the ends of Being and ideal Grace.
I love thee to the level of everyday's
Most quiet need, by sun and candle-light.
I love thee freely, as men strive for Right;
I love thee purely, as they turn from Praise.
I love thee with the passion put to use
In my old griefs, and with my childhood's faith.
I love thee with a love I seemed to lose
With my lost saints, – I love thee with the breath,
Smiles, tears, of all my life! – and if God choose,
I shall but love thee better after death.

'To my Dear and Loving Husband':
Anne Bradstreet (1612–72)*

If ever two were one, then surely we.
If ever man were loved by wife, then thee;
If ever wife was happy in a man,
Compare with me, ye women, if you can.
I prize thy love more than whole mines of gold
Or all the riches that the East doth hold.
My love is such that rivers cannot quench,
Nor ought but love from thee, give recompense.
Thy love is such I can no way repay,

The heavens reward thee manifold, I pray.
The while we live, in love let's so persevere,
That when we live no more, we may live ever.

'Letter to Dafnis', 2 April 1685: Anne Finch, Countess of Winchilsea (1661–1720)*

This to the Crown, and blessing of my life,
The much lov'd husband, of a happy wife.
To him, whose constant passion found the art
To win a stubborn, and ungrateful heart;
And to the World, by tend'rest proof discovers
They err, who say that husbands can't be lovers.
With such return of passion, as is due,
Daphnis I love, Daphnis my thoughts persue,
Daphnis, my hopes, my joys are bounded all in you:
Ev'n I, for Daphnis, and my promise sake,
What I in women censure, undertake.
But this from love, not vanity proceeds;
You know who writes; and I who 'tis that reads.
Judge not my passion, by my want of skill,
Many love well, though they express itt ill;
And I your censure cou'd with pleasure bear,
Wou'd you but soon return, and speak itt here.

'My True Love Hath My Heart': Sir Philip Sidney (1554–86)

My true-love hath my heart, and I have his,
By just exchange one for another given:
I hold his dear, and mine he cannot miss,
There never was a better bargain driven:
　　My true-love hath my heart, and I have his.

My heart in me keeps him and me in one,
My heart in him his thoughts and senses guide:
He loves my heart, for once it was his own,
I cherish his because in me it bides:
   My true-love hath my heart, and I have his.

'Love': Rowena Edlin-White*

You love me very much.
How do I know this?
Because you take me as I am,
The whole package,
Without reservation:
The veins in my legs,
The lines on my face,
The grey in my hair,
And love me anyway.

You love me very hard.
How can I be so sure?
Because you read my heart,
The whole story,
And don't hold back:
My barrenness,
My cowardice,
My poverty of spirit,
And love me anyway.

You love me very dearly.
How do you do it?
You don't care what they say
Behind our backs:
My crazy clothes,
My unashamed middle-aged,
Irreverent, outrageous,

Blooming sensuality!
You take it all in your stride,
You love me anyway.

The bridegroom speaks of his wife

*'The Good-Morrow': John Donne (c.1571–1631)**

The lovers described in this poem are so absorbed by each other that they feel they are alone in their own world. They have confidence in the strength of their love, knowing it will last.

I wonder by my troth, what thou, and I
Did, till we lov'd? were we not wean'd till then?
But, suck'd on countrey pleasures, childishly?
Or snorted we i'the seaven sleepers den?
'Twas so; But this, all pleasures fancies bee.
If ever any beauty I did see,
Which I desir'd, and got, 'twas but a dreame of thee.

And now good morrow to our waking soules,
Which watch not one another out of feare;
For love, all love of other sights controules,
And makes one little roome, an every where.
Let sea-discoverers to new worlds have gone,
Let Maps to others, worlds on worlds have showne,
let us possesse our world, each hath one, and is one.

My face in thine eye, thine in mine appeares,
And true plaine hearts doe in the faces rest,
Where can we finde two better hemispheres
Without sharpe North, without declining West?
What ever dyes, was not mixt equally;

If our two loves be one, or, thou and I
Love so alike, that none doe slacken, none can die.

'A Dedication to my Wife': T. S. Eliot (1888–1965)*

To whom I owe the leaping delight
That quickens my senses in our wakingtime
And the rhythm that governs the repose of our sleeping-
    time,
        The breathing in unison

Of lovers whose bodies smell of each other
Who think the same thoughts without need of speech
And babble the same speech without need of meaning.

No peevish winter wind shall chill
No sullen tropic sun shall wither
The roses in the rose-garden which is ours and ours only

But this dedication is for others to read:
These are my private words addressed to you in public.

'The Confirmation': Edwin Muir (1887–1959)*

Yes, yours, my love, is the right human face.
I in my mind had waited for this long,
Seeing the false and searching for the true,
Then found you as a traveller finds a place
Of welcome suddenly amid the wrong
Valleys and rocks and twisting roads. But you,
What shall I call you? A fountain in a waste,
A well of water in a country dry,
Or anything that's honest and good, an eye
That makes the whole world bright. Your open heart,
Simple with giving, gives the primal deed,

107

The first good world, the blossom, the blowing seed,
The heart, the steadfast land, the wandering sea,
Not beautiful or rare in every part,
But like yourself, as they were meant to be.

'Reprise': Ogden Nash (1902–71)

Geniuses of countless nations
Have told their love for generations
Till all their memorable phrases
Are common as goldenrod or daisies.
Their girls have glimmered like the moon,
Or shimmered like a summer noon,
Stood like a lily, fled like fawn,
Now the sunset, now the dawn,
Here the princess in the tower
There the sweet forbidden flower.
Darling, when I look at you
Every aged phrase is new,
And there are moments when it seems
I've married one of Shakespeare's dreams.

9

Music

~~~~~~◆~~~~~~

Who plays the music?

There are normally three categories of music required during a wedding: coming in and going out of the church (called processional and recessional respectively), hymns sung during the service, and music played during the signing of the register. Additionally, you might also like some music during Communion if your marriage has a Eucharistic setting. How the music is chosen will depend upon your own taste and on who is available to provide the accompaniment. The whole thing could be left to the church organist, or you may have friends and contacts of your own who are willing to take part. Organs are not readily found in hotels or gardens, but an electric organ or piano might be substituted; and while there probably won't be room in most parish churches for an entire chamber orchestra, there could be out of doors! In church or elsewhere, if you know someone involved in orchestral music, a brass or silver band, a string quartet, early music consort or even a jazz ensemble, why not ask them?

Organist (or pianist)

If you would like the resident church organist to play, make sure you know how much you will be paying him or her (sometimes it is included in the overall fee, but not always), and speak to them well in advance. If you want to bring in your own accompanist there shouldn't be any problem, so long as everyone understands what the arrangements are. There may be a small charge for use of the organ, and theoretically the resident organist is entitled to the standard fee regardless of who actually plays it, but most will waive the fee if not playing themselves. Remember, an outsider will probably want to practise *in situ*, so this must be arranged.

Choirs

Some churches – but by no means all – have their own choir. If there is a choir, and you want them to sing at your wedding, you will usually have to pay them. Check out how many of them there are and how much they cost per head before you commit yourselves; it's worth hearing them sing at a service, too, before you decide. One advantage of a choir is that they will lead the singing and create enough sound so that your guests don't feel embarrassed about joining in; they also provide a clear indication of when the congregation should stand or sit.

There's nothing to stop you providing your own, of course. Do you or any of your friends or family sing in a choir or a light operatic group? Maybe one of you is a teacher – why not enlist the school choir? I should keep the numbers to a reasonable level, though; check how much room there is in the church and where they are going to stand if the choir stalls have been removed. If you require the church organist to accompany an outside choir you will need to liaise with both sides as a rehearsal will almost certainly be needed, music agreed upon and exchanged, etc.

Some churches may have a modern 'worship group' who are used to leading livelier hymns and praise songs. Often they include piano and guitars, brass or wind instruments, and even a drum kit. If you have heard them play and would like them at your wedding, approach their leader or musical director to discuss the possibilities. These groups tend to be looser-knit than formal choirs and not necessarily available for extra services, but may be delighted to be asked.

Soloists

A friend or relative who plays a solo instrument or sings well could strike just the right note at certain points in the service. Strings or woodwind are highly suitable for the classical touch but a trombone, saxophone or similar instrument might be more to your taste. I suggest you only choose someone with a high standard of accomplishment and discipline: little cousin Mary may be charming on her flute at the Christmas party but may not be confident or reliable enough to perform in the context of a church service!

Taped music

Churches have not yet realized the full potential for using taped music in services but there is no reason why you shouldn't use it if you want it, subject to the minister's approval. It is not a good idea for accompanying singing, but is ideal for playing as guests arrive, for the processional, and later for the recessional as the wedding party leave church. Do check out the quality of the church's sound equipment or provide a compatible tape or CD deck of your own, and make sure you have somebody reliable to operate it – perhaps one of your ushers might take charge.

Choosing your music

Music is highly evocative and can set the whole tone of the proceedings. If you want to create an air of dignified ceremonial, then you can't beat good organ music, traditional hymns and maybe a classical solo. For something more informal and lively, jazz or electric instruments, modern praise songs and a worship group singing during the service are more appropriate. Decide on the 'feel' of your service, then go for music you like and feel comfortable with, keeping in mind that music in church is supposed to have some reference to, or at least respect for, God; so one kind might be more suitable than another. If in doubt, have a chat with whoever co-ordinates the church music. If you really have no idea what you want, or you can't remember the name of that lively wedding march your friend Jane had, they will certainly be able to make some suggestions. Some organists even have a tape of their own repertoire which they lend to wedding couples to choose from, or you may find compilations of popular church music in the library.

Processionals and recessionals

There are a number of very popular organ pieces which are suitable for either processionals or recessionals and most organists will know them. Not all of them, though, will be able to play them, so do check that out. It is a good idea to choose something slower for the processional – everyone will want a good look at the bridal party as they enter – and a more energetic, joyful piece for the recessional.

Popular pieces

Arrival of the Queen of Sheba – Handel
Bridal March from 'Lohengrin' – Wagner
Crown Imperial – Walton
Grand March from 'Aida' – Verdi
Overture to the Royal Fireworks Music – Handel
Trumpet Voluntary – Jeremiah Clarke
Trumpet Tune and Air – Purcell
Hornpipe in F from the Water Music – Handel
Toccata (Symphony no. 5) – Widor
The Wedding March from 'A Midsummer Night's Dream' –
    Mendelssohn
Ode to Joy – Beethoven

Lesser-known pieces

Bridal March from 'The Birds' (music for the stage play by
    Aristophanes, 1883) – Charles Hubert Parry
Canon in D – Pachelbel
Chorale (Now thank we all our God) – Karg-Elert
Litanies – Alain Jehan
Molde Canticle Part 1 – Jan Garbarek
Prince of Denmark's March – Jeremiah Clarke
Rigadoon – Handel
Te Deum – Marc-Antoine Charpentier

Of course you don't have to come in and go out to an organ piece. If there is a choir a short choral piece such as 'I Was Glad' (Parry) or 'Zadok the Priest' (Handel) could be used; if you have jazz instruments, 'When the Saints Go Marching

In' or something in that vein would provide a celebratory note to exit with.

Hymns as processionals and recessionals

A good, up-beat hymn, preferably with a rousing chorus, can serve just as well as a wedding march if there is a choir or you can rely on your guests to sing out. Indeed, if you dread the thought of every eye glued upon you as you enter, a hymn is just the thing to divert attention!

A good tip: choose something with no more than four or five verses, or leave some out – it doesn't take too long to process down most aisles!

Traditional favourites[1]

All people that on earth do dwell (William Kethe 1520–94)
Jesus Christ is risen today, hallelujah! (*Lyra Davidica* 1708)
Now thank we all our God (Martin Rinkart 1586–1649, tr. Catherine Winkworth 1829–78)
O for a thousand tongues to sing (Charles Wesley 1707–88)
Thine be the glory, risen conquering Son (Edmond Budry 1854–1932, tr. R. Birch Hoyle 1875–1939)
To God be the glory (Frances von Alstyne 1820–1915)

Modern hymns

Jesus is Lord! (David J. Mansell)
Lord of Lords, King of Kings (Jessy Dixon, Randy Scruggs & John Thompson)

1. All hymns are listed, with sources, at the end of this chapter, so if you cannot easily lay hands on them, your organist should be able to locate them.

Rejoice! rejoice! (Graham Kendrick)
Shine, Jesus, shine (Lord the light of your love is shining)
  (Graham Kendrick)
Tell out, my soul (Timothy Dudley-Smith)
You shall go out with joy (Stuart Dauermann)

Other ideas

A solo instrument or voice can be very calming and effective
as the bride or couple enter the church. This will depend
largely upon the repertoire of your soloist who may be able
to offer some suggestions. 'Panis Angelicus', made popular
by the TV serial 'The Choir', is well-known and could be
sung by a solo treble or choir to good effect.

The author was once asked to sing a setting of Psalm 108
which had been composed by the bride; if either of you
have the gift, why not compose a piece especially for your
wedding?

A recording of an early music consort playing a stately
pavane or other tune would provide an historic flavour. Lute
music, lilting and bubbling, would also be effective.

If you have a Morris Dance or Folk Dance connection, the
bridal party could be escorted in and out by the team playing and dancing a suitable tune. This would be particularly
appropriate for an outside venue.

Why not do something completely different and enter in
perfect silence?

Hymns

Leaving aside the processional and recessional hymns, there are usually two or three hymns. One normally occurs immediately after the entrance of the bride and before the marriage, the second after the marriage and the last at the end of the service. The first ought to be a hymn of praise to God in whose presence the company is met; the second might be either a burst of joy and praise to celebrate the union which has just taken place, or it could be something more meditative, depending on how you feel. If you are signing the register at this point I suggest the latter, to be followed by some other music or a solo (see the section 'During the signing of the register', below). The final hymn, whether used as a recessional or not, ought to be up-beat, familiar and joyful. Of course, you can vary any of these to suit yourselves.

Choosing your hymns

Each church has its own favourite hymn book which may or may not contain the hymns you want; *Mission Praise, Hymns Ancient & Modern, Songs of Fellowship, (Methodist) Hymns and Psalms* and *The New English Hymnal* are all currently in use and contain a mixture of old and new. There are several others. Ask to borrow a copy at an early planning stage; chances are the organist or pianist will be familiar with the contents and have the music edition. If not, you may have to supply the music for what you choose. Agree with the accompanist which tune will be used if there are several. Choose at least one well-known hymn or one with an easy tune which can be picked up quickly; remember, you may be too preoccupied yourself to sing out and give a lead – this is where a choir comes in handy! Also, do read the words carefully: 'Dear Lord and Father of Mankind' is a splendid old hymn but the second line, 'forgive our foolish ways', is not especially suitable for a wedding – some wag is bound to pick up on it!

Some suggestions follow; if the words appeal but you can't recall the tunes, ask the organist to run through them for you. Also, you may find the language has in some cases been updated, so you will have to decide whether you prefer this or the original.

Hymns of praise to God

These hymns acknowledge God as creator and sustainer of all things, thanking him for his goodness to, and his continual provision for us.

1. All creatures of our God and king
lift up your voice and with us sing
    Alleluia, alleluia!
Bright burning sun with golden beam,
soft shining moon with silver gleam,
    O praise him, O praise him,
    Alleluia, alleluia, alleluia!

2. Swift rushing wind so wild and strong,
white clouds that sail in heaven along,
    O praise him, alleluia!
New rising dawn in praise rejoice,
you lights of evening find a voice;
    O praise him ...

3. Cool flowing water, pure and clear,
make music for your Lord to hear,
    Alleluia, alleluia!
Fierce fire so masterful and bright

giving to us both warmth and light,
  O praise him ...

4. People and nations, take your part,
love and forgive with all your heart.
  Alleluia, alleluia!
All who long pain and sorrow bear,
trust God and cast on him your care;
  O praise him ...

5. Let all things their creator bless
and worship him in lowliness:
  Alleluia, alleluia!
Praise, praise the Father, praise the Son,
and praise the Spirit, Three-in-One,
  O praise him ...

> After St Francis of Assisi, William Henry Draper
> (1855–1933); © in this version Jubilate Hymns

All things bright and beautiful,
all creatures great and small,
all things wise and wonderful –
the Lord God made them all.

1. Each little flower that opens,
each little bird that sings –
he made their glowing colours,
he made their tiny wings.
  All things bright ...

2. The purple-headed mountain,
the river running by,
the sunset, and the morning
that brightens up the sky:
  All things bright ...

118

3. The cold wind in the winter,
the pleasant summer sun,
the ripe fruits in the garden –
he made them every one.
    All things bright ...

4. He gave us eyes to see them,
and lips that we might tell
how great is God almighty,
who has made all things well!
    All things bright ...

Cecil Frances Alexander (1818–95)

1. Bring to the Lord a glad new song,
children of grace, extol your king;
worship and praise to God belong –
to instruments of music, sing!
Let those be warned who spurn his name;
nations and kings, attend his word;
God's justice shall bring tyrants shame:
let every creature praise the Lord!

2. Praise him within these hallowed walls,
praise him beneath the dome of heaven;
by cymbals' sounds and trumpets' calls
let praises fit for God be given:
with strings and brass and wind rejoice –
then, join his praise with full accord
all living things with breath and voice:
let every creature praise the Lord!

From Psalms 149 & 150; © Michael Perry/ Jubilate Hymns

1. For the beauty of the earth,
for the beauty of the skies,
for the love which from our birth
over and around us lies,
  Christ our God, to you we raise
  this our sacrifice of praise.

2. For the beauty of each hour
of the day and of the night,
hill and vale, and tree and flower,
sun and moon and stars of light,
  Christ our God ...

3. For the joy of ear and eye,
for the heart and mind's delight,
for the mystic harmony
linking sense to sound and sight,
  Christ our God ...

4. For the joy of human love,
brother, sister, parent, child,
friends on earth and friends above,
pleasures pure and undefiled,
  Christ our God ...

5. For each perfect gift divine
to our race so freely given,
joys bestowed by love's design,
flowers of earth and fruits of heaven,
  Christ our God ...

Folliott Sandford Pierpoint (1835–1917)

1. Great is your faithfulness, O God my Father,
you have fulfilled all your promise to me;
you never fail and your love is unchanging –
all you have been you for ever will be.
Great is your faithfulness, great is your faithfulness;
morning by morning new mercies I see;
all I have needed your hand has provided –
great is your faithfulness, Father, to me!

2. Summer and winter, and springtime and harvest,
sun, moon and stars in their courses above
join with all nature in eloquent witness
to your great faithfulness, mercy and love.
Great is your faithfulness...

3. Pardon for sin, and a peace everlasting,
your living presence to cheer and to guide;
strength for today, and bright hope for tomorrow –
these are the blessings your love will provide.
Great is your faithfulness...

T. O. Chisholm (1866–1960) Administered by CopyCare, P.O. Box 77,
Hailsham, BN27 3EF, UK. Used by permission. With grateful thanks
to Jubilate Hymns for modernizing the lyrics.

1. Let all the world in every corner sing,
    'My God and King!'
The heavens are not too high,
his praise may thither fly;
the earth is not too low,
his praises there may grow:
let all the world in every corner sing,
    'My God and King!'

2. Let all the world in every corner sing,
    'My God and King!'

The church with psalms must shout –
no door can keep them out;
but above all, the heart
must bear the longest part:
let all the world in every corner sing,
  'My God and King!'

George Herbert (1593–1632)

1. O God beyond all praising, we worship you today
and sing the love amazing that songs cannot repay;
for we can only wonder at every gift you send,
at blessings without number and mercies without end:
we lift our hearts before you and wait upon your word,
we honour and adore you, our great and mighty Lord.

2. Then hear, O gracious Saviour,
  accept the love we bring,
that we who know your favour may serve you as our king;
and whether our tomorrows be filled with good or ill,
we'll triumph through our sorrows
  and rise to bless you still:
to marvel at your beauty and glory in your ways,
and make a joyful duty our sacrifice of praise!

© Michael Perry/ Jubilate Hymns

1. Praise, my soul, the king of heaven!
To his feet your tribute bring:
ransomed, healed, restored, forgiven,
who like me his praise should sing?
  Alleluia, alleluia!
  praise the everlasting king!

2. Praise him for his grace and favour
to his people in distress;
praise him still the same for ever,

slow to chide and swift to bless:
   Alleluia, alleluia!
   glorious in his faithfulness!

3. Father-like, he tends and spares us;
all our hopes and fears he knows,
in his hands he gently bears us,
rescues us from all our foes,
   Alleluia, alleluia!
   widely as his mercy flows.

4. Angels, help us to adore him –
you behold him face to face;
sun and moon, bow down before him –
praise him, all in time and space:
   Alleluia, alleluia!
   praise with us the God of grace!

From Psalm 103; Henry Francis Lyte (1793–1847)

1. Tell out, my soul, the greatness of the Lord!
Unnumbered blessings, give my spirit voice;
tender to me the promise of his word –
In God my saviour shall my heart rejoice.

2. Tell out, my soul, the greatness of his name!
Make known his might, the deeds his arm has done;
his mercy sure, from age to age the same –
his holy name: the Lord, the mighty one.

3. Tell out, my soul, the greatness of his might!
Powers and dominions lay their glory by;
proud hearts and stubborn wills are put to flight,
the hungry fed, the humble lifted high.

4. Tell out, my soul, the glories of his word!
Firm is his promise, and his mercy sure:
tell out, my soul, the greatness of the Lord
to children's children and for evermore!

> From Luke 1, the Magnificat; © Timothy Dudley-Smith

1. To God be the glory! Great things he has done;
so loved he the world that he gave us his Son
who yielded his life an atonement for sin,
and opened the life-gate that all may go in.
> Praise the Lord, praise the Lord!
> let the earth hear his voice;
> Praise the Lord, praise the Lord!
> let the people rejoice:
> O come to the Father through Jesus the Son
> and give him the glory – great things he has done.

2. O perfect redemption, the purchase of blood!
To every believer the promise of God:
the vilest offender who truly believes,
that moment from Jesus a pardon receives.
> Praise the Lord ...

3. Great things he has taught us, great things he has done,
and great our rejoicing through Jesus the Son:
but purer and higher and greater will be
our wonder, our gladness, when Jesus we see!
> Praise the Lord ...

> Frances van Alstyne (1820–1915)

Other suggestions

Hallelujah! Sing to Jesus (William Chatterton Dix 1837–98)

Jesus is Lord! (David J. Mansell)

Morning has broken (Eleanor Farjeon 1881–1965)

Now thank we all our God (Martin Rinkart 1586–1649, tr. Catherine Winkworth 1828–78)

Let us with a gladsome mind (John Milton 1608–74)

O for a thousand tongues to sing (Charles Wesley 1707–88)

O Lord my God! When I in awesome wonder (Stuart K. Hine 1899–1989)

Praise to the Lord, the Almighty (Joachim Neander 1650–80, tr. Catherine Winkworth 1829–78)

Hymns of love

Hymns and songs about the love of God for his creation, or the self-sacrificing love of Jesus, are appropriate for weddings as they speak of some of the qualities needed to sustain the new relationship. Any of these, or the 'Hymns of Hope' following, would be suitable for a second hymn, or the last hymn where it was not the recessional.

1. Come down, O Love divine!
Seek out this soul of mine
and visit it with your own ardour glowing;
O Comforter, draw near,
within my heart appear,
and kindle it, your holy flame bestowing.

2. O let it freely burn
till earthly passions turn
to dust and ashes in its heat consuming;
and let your glorious light
shine ever on my sight,
and make my pathway clear, by your illuming.

3. Let holy charity
my outward vesture be,
and lowliness become my inner clothing;
true lowliness of heart
which takes the humbler part,
and for its own shortcomings weeps with loathing.

4. And so the yearning strong
with which the soul will long
shall far surpass the power of human telling;
for none can guess its grace
till we become the place
in which the Holy Spirit makes his dwelling.
Richard F. Littledale (1833–90) © in this version Jubilate Hymns

1. **Love came down at Christmas**
Love all lovely, Love divine;
Love was born at Christmas,
star and angels gave the sign.

2. Worship we the Godhead,
Love incarnate, Love divine;
worship we our Jesus:
but wherewith for sacred sign?

3. Love shall be our token,
love be yours and love be mine,
love to God and all men (*or* all of us),
love for plea and gift and sign.

Christina Rossetti (1830–94)

1. Love divine, all loves excelling,
joy of heaven, to earth come down:
fix in us your humble dwelling,
all your faithful mercies crown.

2. Jesus, you are all compassion,
pure, unbounded love impart:
visit us with your salvation,
enter every trembling heart.

3. Come, almighty to deliver,
let us all your grace receive;
suddenly return, and never,
never more your temples leave.

4. We would always give you blessing,
serve you as your hosts above,
pray, and praise you without ceasing,
glory in your perfect love.

5. Finish then your new creation:
pure and spotless let us be;
let us see your great salvation,
perfect in eternity:

6. Changed from glory into glory
till in heaven we take our place,
there to sing salvation's story,
lost in wonder, love and praise!

Charles Wesley (1707–88) © in this version
Word & Music/Jubilate Hymns

1. O perfect Love, all human thought transcending,
lowly we kneel in prayer before your throne,
that you will give the love which knows no ending,
to those whom evermore you join in one.

2. O perfect Love, become their full assurance
of tender love and steadfast godly faith,
of patient hope, and quiet brave endurance,
with childlike trust that fears not pain or death.

3. Grant them the joy that lightens earthly sorrow,
grant them the peace that calms all earthly strife;
and to life's day the glorious bright tomorrow
that dawns upon eternal love and life.

Dorothy F. Gurney (1858–1932) this version
Words & Music/ Jubilate Hymns

1. **The king of love my shepherd is,**
whose goodness fails me never;
I nothing lack if I am his
and he is mine for ever.

2. Where streams of living water flow
a ransomed soul, he leads me;
and where the fertile pastures grow,
with food from heaven feeds me.

3. Perverse and foolish I have strayed,
but in his love he sought me;
and on his shoulder gently laid,
and home, rejoicing, brought me.

4. In death's dark vale I fear no ill
with you, dear Lord, beside me;
your rod and staff my comfort still,
your cross before to guide me.

5. You spread a banquet in my sight
of love beyond all knowing;
and O the gladness and delight
from your pure chalice flowing!

6. And so through all the length of days
your goodness fails me never:
Good Shepherd, may I sing your praise
within your house for ever!

From Psalm 23, Henry Williams Baker (1821–77)
© in this version Jubilate Hymns

Other suggestions
Amazing grace (John Newton 1725–1807)
From heaven you came, helpless babe/The Servant King
(Graham Kendrick)
God is love: let heaven adore Him (Timothy Rees
1874–1939)
How precious, O Lord, is your unfailing love (Phil Rogers)
O love of God, how strong and true! (Horatius Bonar
1808–89)
O Love that wilt not let me go (George Matheson
1842–1906)
O the deep, deep love of Jesus! (Samuel Trevor Francis
1834–1925)

So freely flows the endless love you give to me (Dave
  Bilbrough)
Such love (Graham Kendrick)

Hymns of hope

Other hymns speak of the desire that God will go with us
into the future and help us to live out the promises we have
just made.

> 1. Father, hear the prayer we offer:
> not for ease that prayer shall be,
> but for strength, that we may ever
> live our lives courageously.
>
> 2. Not for ever in green pastures
> do we ask our way to be:
> but by steep and rugged pathways
> would we strive to climb to Thee.
>
> 3. Not for ever by still waters
> would we idly quiet stray;
> but would smite the living fountains
> from the rocks along our way.
>
> 4. Be our strength in hours of weakness,
> in our wanderings be our guide;
> through endeavour, failure, danger,
> Father, be Thou at our side.
>
> 5. Let our path be bright or dreary,
> storm or sunshine be our share;
> may our souls, in hope unweary,
> make Thy work our ceaseless prayer.
>
> Love Maria Willis (1824–1908)

1. Lead us, heavenly Father, lead us
   o'er the world's tempestuous sea;
guard us, guide us, keep us, feed us –
   for we have no help but thee,
yet possessing every blessing
   if our God our Father be.

2. Saviour, breathe forgiveness o'er us:
   all our weakness thou dost know,
thou didst tread this earth before us,
   thou didst feel its keenest woe;
lone and dreary, faint and weary,
   through the desert thou didst go.

3. Spirit of our God, descending,
   fill our hearts with heavenly joy,
love with every passion blending,
   pleasure that can never cloy:
thus provided, pardoned, guided,
   nothing can our peace destroy.

James Edmeston (1791–1867)

1. Lord, for the years your love has kept and guided,
urged and inspired us, cheered us on our way,
sought us and saved us, pardoned and provided,
Lord of the years, we bring our thanks today.

2. Lord, for that word, the word of life which fires us,
speaks to our hearts and sets our souls ablaze;
teaches and trains, rebukes us and inspires us;
Lord of the word, receive your people's praise.

3. Lord, for our land, in this our generation,
spirits oppressed by pleasure, wealth and care;
for young and old, for commonwealth and nation,
Lord of our land, be pleased to hear our prayer.

4. Lord, for our world; when we disown and doubt him,
loveless in strength, and comfortless in pain;
hungry and helpless, lost indeed without him;
Lord of the world, we pray that Christ may reign.

5. Lord, for ourselves, in living power remake us –
self on the cross and Christ upon the throne,
past put behind us, for the future take us,
Lord of our lives, to live for Christ alone.

© Timothy Dudley-Smith

1. Lord Jesus Christ, invited guest and saviour,
with tender mercy hear us as we pray;
grant our desire for those who seek your favour,
come with your love and bless them both today.

2. Give them your strength for caring and for serving,
give them your graces – faithfulness and prayer;
make their resolve to follow you unswerving,
make their reward your peace beyond compare.

3. Be their delight in joy, their hope in sorrow,
be their true friend in pleasure as in pain;
guest of today and guardian of tomorrow,
turn humble water into wine again!

© Michael Perry/ Jubilate Hymns

1. May the mind of Christ our saviour
live in us from day to day,
by his love and power controlling
all we do or say.

2. May the word of God enrich us
with his truth from hour to hour;
so that all may know we triumph
only through his power.

3. May the peace of God our Father
in our lives for ever reign,
that we may be calm to comfort
those in grief and pain.

4. May the love of Jesus fill us,
as the waters fill the sea,
him exhalting, self abasing –
this is victory!

5. May his beauty rest upon us
as we seek to make him known;
so that all may look to Jesus,
seeing him alone.

Kate B. Wilkinson (1859–1928) © in this version
Word & Music/ Jubilate Hymns

Other suggestions

Bind us together, Lord (Bob Gillman)
Blest be the tie that binds (John Fawcett 1740–1817)
Jesus stand among us at the meeting of our lives (Graham
    Kendrick)
Jesus the Lord of love and life (James E. Seddon)
Living under the shadow of His wing (David J. Hadden and
    Bob Silvester)
Make me a channel of your peace (Sebastian Temple)
New every morning is the love (John Keble 1792–1866)
O Jesus I have promised (John Ernest Bode 1816–74)
You are the vine, we are the branches (Danny Daniels)

During the signing of the register

The register has to be signed at some point in the service; this involves the minister, bride, groom and two witnesses, also a registrar in some churches. The whole process takes five to ten minutes. Often the signing is done near the end of the service, out of sight, in the vestry or ante-room, so the procession out of church begins as the party emerges. However, many people feel that it is nicer to sign in sight of the congregation at a table in the chancel or in a side chapel if there is one, and to do it immediately after the declaration that the couple are husband and wife. That way it is not seen as a hiatus in the proceedings, but an important and necessary part of the service. In or out of sight, it provides an opportunity for the congregation to untense after the excitement of the marriage ceremony; but if they are not to dissolve into inconsequential chit-chat at this point, you need to provide something to cover those few minutes which will be pleasurable, uplifting and in keeping with the proceedings. Music is the obvious solution and a number of alternatives are listed below:

An organ piece could be played:
Adagio – Albinoni
Humoresque – P. A. Yon

Another hymn might be inserted here, perhaps timed to begin a couple of minutes before the bridal party return to their places.

If there is a choir, an anthem (or two) could be sung; the musical director will be able to suggest something suitable.

For example:

For the beauty of the earth – John Rutter

Greater Love – John Ireland

My beloved spake – Patrick Hadley

Love one another, from 'Blessed be the God and Father' – Samuel Sebastian Wesley

More informally, a worship group might lead the congregation in a number of modern praise songs (words to be supplied on the service sheet). At one wedding, in a very small church where the register had to be signed 'off-stage', the musical director taught the congregation a simple round, 'Seek ye first the kingdom of God', which was enjoyably sung until the couple returned!

Other suggestions

All heaven declares the glory of the risen Lord (Noel and Tricia Richards)

Be still, for the presence of the Lord (David J. Evans)

Come on and celebrate! (Patricia Morgan)

Give thanks with a grateful heart (Henry Smith)

Great is the Lord and most worthy of praise (Steve McEwan)

Here we are, gathered together as a family (Steve Hampton)

Jesus put this song into our hearts (Graham Kendrick)

Let there be love shared among us (Dave Bilbrough)

Living under the shadow of His wing (David J. Hadden and Bob Silvester)

May the fragrance of Jesus fill this place (Graham Kendrick)

O Lord, your tenderness (Graham Kendrick)

A solo or group instrumental piece – not necessarily a 'classical' piece either; a string or wind ensemble is ideal but

Spanish guitar or brass instruments have all been employed to good effect in the past!

A solo vocal piece (or two) if you have people available, for example:

The Lord is my Shepherd – Charles Villiers Stanford or various other settings

Ave Maria – various settings

Come Lord Jesus with healing hands – Diane Davis Andrew

Et Exultavit from *Magnificat* – J. S. Bach

Jesu, joy of man's desiring – J. S. Bach

Pie Jesu – Andrew Lloyd Webber

Take my life and let it be (Frances Ridley Havergal 1836–79)

Why not a classical dancer or dancers if there is enough room and you have the connections? Something flowing and lyrical in either balletic or modern dance style would be effective.

Taped music would be perfectly acceptable.

During Communion

Some of the suggestions for the signing of the register would be equally suitable during Holy Communion though the mood should be kept quiet and meditative. Hymns or praise songs would not help the atmosphere, but a solo voice (see solo vocal pieces above) or an appropriate anthem from the choir at some point would be acceptable.

Bells

I will mention bells here because they are, after all, part of the music. Many parish churches have a peal of bells that contributes a very festive air to a wedding. You will almost certainly have to pay for the privilege – anything from £45 to £200 depending on how many ringers are required. A few churches use a tape over a PA system and presumably this does not incur the same sort of expense. The minister should provide you with a list of fees when you first meet anyway, so you can decide what will fit into your budget.

Some sources of hymns mentioned

Key
A&M: Hymns Ancient & Modern, New Standard Edition
BPW: Baptist Praise & Worship
H&P: (Methodist) Hymns & Psalms
HFP: Hymns for the People
HTC: Hymns for Today's Church
MP: Mission Praise
NEH: New English Hymnal
SF: Songs of Fellowship

All creatures of our God and king A&M; BPW; H&P; HFP; HTC; MP; NEH
All heaven declares MP; SF
All people that on earth do dwell A&M; BPW; H&P; HFP; HTC; SF; MP; NEH
All things bright and beautiful A&M; BPW; H&P; HFP; HTC; MP; NEH; SF
Amazing grace BPW; H&P; HFP; HTC; MP; SF
Be still, for the presence of the Lord BPW; HFP; MP; SF

Bind us together, Lord BPW; HTC; MP; SF;

Blest be the tie that binds BPW; H&P; MP; SF

Bring to the Lord a glad new song BPW; HFP; HTC

Come down, O Love divine! A&M; BPW; H&P; HFP; HTC; MP; NEH

Come on and celebrate! MP; SF

Father, hear the prayer we offer A&M; BPW; H&P; HEH; HTC; MP; SF

For the beauty of the earth A&M; BPW; H&P; HFP; HTC; MP; NEH

From heaven you came, helpless babe/The Servant King BPW; HFP; MP; SF

Give thanks with a grateful heart MP; SF

God is love: let heaven adore him A&M; BPW; H&P; MP; NEH

Great is your faithfulness, O God my Father BPW; H&P; HFP; HTC; MP; SF

Great is the Lord and most worthy of praise MP; SF

Hallelujah! Sing to Jesus MP; SF

Here we are, gathered together/The Family Song SF

How precious, O Lord, is your unfailing love MP; SF

Jesus Christ is risen today, Hallelujah! A&M; BPW; HFP; HTC; MP; NEH; SF

Jesus is Lord! BPW; H&P; HTC; MP; SF

Jesus put this song into our hearts MP; SF

Jesus stand among us at the meeting of our lives MP; SF

Jesus the Lord of love and life BPW

Lead us, heavenly Father, lead us A&M; BPW; H&P; HFP; HTC; MP; NEH; SF

Let all the world in every corner sing A&M; BPW; H&P; HTC; MP; NEH

Let there be love shared among us BPW; MP; SF

Let us with a gladsome mind A&M; H&P; HTC; MP; NEH; SF

Living under the shadow of His wing MP; SF

Lord, for the years BPW; HFP; HTC; MP

Lord Jesus Christ, invited guest HTC

Lord of Lords, King of Kings SF

Lord, the light of your love is shining/Shine Jesus, shine BPW; HFP; MP; SF

Love came down at Christmas BPW; H&P; MP; SF

Love divine, all loves excelling A&M; BPW; H&P; HFP; HTC; MP

Make me a channel of your peace BPW; H&P; HFP; HTC; MP; SF

May the fragrance of Jesus fill this place MP; SF

May the mind of Christ our Saviour BPW; H&P; HFP; HTC; MP

Morning has broken BPW; H&P; HFP; HTC; MP; NEH; SF

New every morning is the love A&M; H&P; HFP; HTC; MP; NEH

Now thank we all our God A&M; BPW; H&P; HFP; HTC; MP; NEH; SF

O for a thousand tongues to sing MP;

O God beyond all praising HFP; HTC

O Jesus I have promised A&M; BPW; H&P; HFP; HTC; MP; NEH; SF

O Lord my God, when I in awesome wonder BPW; MP; SF

O Lord, your tenderness MP; SF

O love of God, how strong and true! BPW; MP; H&P

O Love that wilt not let me go BPW; H&P; HFP; HTC; MP; SF

O perfect love, all human thought transcending A&M; BPW; H&P; MP; NEH

Oh the deep, deep love of Jesus! HTC; MP

Praise, my soul, the king of heaven A&M; BPW; H&P; HFP; HTC; MP; NEH; SF

Rejoice! rejoice! HFP; MP; SF

Seek ye first the kingdom of God BPW; H&P; MP; SF

So freely flows the endless love MP; SF

Such love HFP; MP; SF

Take my life and let it be A&M; BPW; H&P; HFP; HTC; MP; SF

Tell out my soul A&M; BPW; H&P; HFP; HTC; MP; NEH; SF

The king of love my shepherd is A&M; BPW; H&P; HFP; HTC; MP; NEH; SF

Thine be the glory, risen, conquering Son A&M; H&P; HFP; HTC; MP; NEH; SF

To God be the glory BPW; H&P; HFP; HTC; MP; SF

You are the vine, we are the branches MP; SF

You shall go out with joy MP; SF

10

Putting it All Together

~~~~~<><>~~~~~

*I*n a sense, your wedding began the day you decided
to get married and then first approached the
registrar or minister. Lots of ideas will have been
bounced around and no doubt some will have been dis-
carded along the way, but the time eventually comes for
them all to be drawn together into that short space of time
which will be the service, ceremony, blessing, or combina-
tion of these which marks your marriage. Remember,
your commitment to one another is already in place; the
ceremony is not a magical transformation, nor is it merely a
formality or a legal requirement. It is a public declaration of
intent, blessed by God, before a gathering of people who are
important to you.

Timing

Previous chapters have given guidelines on the legal
requirements. Licence, banns or certificate, in consultation
with minister or registrar, should be top of your list at least
three months before your wedding day – though do check as
some requirements are currently being reviewed and could
change. We have looked at how the verbal part of the service

is put together and you should decide on prayers and readings in plenty of time – say, six weeks before – and notify those involved. Music, including hymns, processional, recessional and any other incidental music also ought to be organized well in advance and all the necessary people consulted for availability. Give yourselves as much time as possible so there are no last minute panics on discovering the banns haven't been read in all the right places, or the organist has gone on holiday. You will find a useful checklist in Appendix 1, p. 154. All the component parts of your wedding ceremony will gradually begin to fit into place, rather like a jigsaw, to form the picture you want. What follows are a few other things you will need to consider.

Invitations

For most of your guests it all begins with an invitation to join you to celebrate your marriage at such-and-such a place on such-and-such a date. Traditionally, if the bride's parents are footing the bill, or if she still lives at home, the invitation should come from them:

Mrs and Mrs Joseph Griffiths request the pleasure of the company of __ at the marriage of their daughter Megan with Mr Evan Jones at __, etc.

If the bride's parents are separated they might still decide to join forces for their daughter's wedding and send invitations in both names, though they would probably prefer to be named separately. They may drop the formal titles and just use their Christian names.

Similarly if there is only one parent who is organizing the wedding alone, just their name would appear. In actual fact, not many brides marry from home these days and for any number of reasons would rather, with their partner, send out the invitations themselves, for example:

Megan Griffiths and Evan Jones (*or just* Megan and Evan) request the pleasure of your company to help them celebrate their marriage on __ at __, etc.

Don't forget an address for replies and include directions or map to the church for people who won't know where it is. Your invitation should also include details of where the person is expected to continue celebrating afterwards, either at a reception, evening party or whatever, to avoid embarrassment. There is no need to be formal so long as you supply all the information. For example:

Megan and Evan are getting married! Please come and help us celebrate at __ on __ and afterwards at __.

This sets the tone and people know whether it is going to be a very formal occasion or more easy-going. One couple put: 'Dress: comfortable!' on their invitations. This light-hearted approach was really saying, 'Wear whatever you like – suits and hats aren't obligatory!' In reality, most people like to dress up for a wedding, but in that instance the guests didn't feel they had to go to unnecessary expense, and nobody was going to be offended if Auntie Jean turned up with her green hair and purple DMs. So, you can set the scene by how you word your invitations.

Printing the invitations

So far as printing is concerned, decorated wedding stationery, whilst charming, can be expensive. With a computer and a reasonable desk-top publishing package, you can easily produce your own. Either use your own printer or have the original design photocopied on to good quality card. Alternatively, buy blank invitation cards and use an electric typewriter with a memory facility; this takes a bit longer to feed them all through by hand. You might decorate the results yourself with a dash of glitter or confetti, or stick the cards onto coloured or hand-made paper.

Address cards

While you're using the computer, if you're about to move into a new home together, it can be very helpful to print off some cards giving your new address to hand out at the reception or enclose with your service sheets, especially if you decide not to do the traditional thing so far as names and titles are concerned. If the bride is retaining her maiden name, for instance, or you are combining your surnames, this is a good opportunity to give them an airing and get people used to the idea from the start. For example:

New Address:
Ms Mary Gordon and Mr Mark Smith
15 Yew Tree Way, Nottingham NG8 3BT
Tel: _____

By the way, it is not difficult to combine your surnames in a double-barrelled surname, for example, Gordon-Smith. However, before the marriage ceremony, the groom should arrange with a solicitor a simple deed to the effect that he is changing his name. In theory you can call yourselves what you like but it helps to have a legal document for altering bank accounts, wills, passports, etc. Both bride and groom sign their original name on the register anyway, for example, Mary Gordon and Mark Smith.

Presents

At the point you send out your invitations, you ought to consider what you want to do about wedding presents, because people will ask; it may seem to be nothing to do with the actual ceremony, but it affects your guests and friends, and also says something about your feelings and beliefs. Of course, a young couple starting out into home-making for the first time need all the help they can get, so make a list of all the things you need, including small mundane things like tea-towels as well as a washing machine or dinner service, so guests can choose something within their budget.

If one or both of you has your own home already, you will probably have accumulated the basics by now. Therefore it might be more sensible to ask for monetary donations toward something special: a good dinner service or an item of furniture, for example. Or you might like to waive the personal gifts altogether and request donations to a pet cause, although guests usually like to feel they are contributing in some way to your new life together. One couple combined the two and asked for cash towards a specific item, all moneys over and above the cost of that item would then go towards a rain-forest project. In this way they had something as a personal reminder of their wedding but also the satisfaction of contributing to long-term benefits for others. The preservation of a piece of woodland or a charitable building project – even presenting something to the church where you are married – would all be possibilities. Often these projects can have your names recorded for posterity.

Some people will inevitably bring presents with them on the day and some may get left in the church, so it is a good idea to ask a friend to specifically keep an eye out for this eventuality, gather them up, and deposit them somewhere safe for the rest of the day.

Flowers

We have already mentioned flowers in the context of symbols in Chapter 5. You will almost certainly want to decorate the church or chapel or other venue for your wedding. You have several options here. You can pay an outside florist to come in and attend to everything – namely, planning the bouquets and buttonholes, and the decorations for the altar, bench-ends and table where the register is signed – all to match your overall colour-scheme. This can be very effective, but can be expensive.

However, most churches and chapels have a regular team of experienced 'flower people' who decorate week by week and know how to create the best effects in that particular building. It is worth having a word with whoever is in charge and asking for their advice and help. You could just leave it to them to do what they normally do, or you could pay for the flowers and consult with them as to colour and effect, which they would then arrange specially for you. Mention any unusual ideas you have, such as an archway of flowers over the church door or garlands twining round the pillars; even if they've never done it before, most enthusiastic flower-arrangers will rise to a challenge!

If yours is one of several weddings on the same day you might liaise with the other wedding parties and agree to share the cost. If you can't come to an agreement, your flowers may well have to be put quickly in place just before the service and removed rapidly at the end. Keep that in mind.

Seasonal flowers

You might like to fit in with the flowers appropriate to the church calendar; many churches have a very bare interior during Lent but, come Easter Sunday, fill the church with lilies and other spring flowers. If you are marrying just after Easter you could offer to add to these: cultivated flowers are expensive around this time, but pussy willow boughs, chestnut leaves and all sorts of new spring greenery can look wonderful. Why not carry a bunch of primroses, violets, snowdrops or other wild flowers instead of a formal bouquet, and make buttonholes of the same?

For a Christmas wedding the church could look absolutely stunning with lots of evergreen and berries. Bouquets and buttonholes could also be made of the less prickly greenery – and lots of mistletoe!

Harvest Festival occurs any time between mid-September and mid-October. Go with it! Fruit and vegetables are plentiful and colourful; lots of orange, red and rust-coloured chrysanthemums, sheaves of corn, conkers and branches of autumn leaves, pumpkins – anything you can think of – will give a happy, fruitful note to any church.

At the other extreme, you may prefer the minimalist approach and plump for just one centrepiece on the altar – a sensible consideration for allergy sufferers!

Seating

Traditionally, the bride's family and friends sit on the left-hand side of the church and the groom's on the right. There is no particular reason for this and it can look very unbalanced, not to mention sad, if one partner has few relatives or friends of their own present. Also a number of guests might find themselves in a quandary if they are friends of both partners equally. Personally, I think it's a custom which requires demolishing; your ushers or stewards could do their best to encourage your guests to mingle – though I'm afraid old habits die hard! In register offices, churches where there is no central aisle and more unusual venues this is not so difficult to achieve. Immediate family, if present, sit in the front pews anyway, and can easily get out to join the recessional at the end, if you have planned it that way. If you have any special needs such as wheelchairs or young children in prams or buggies, plan ahead and get your stewards to direct them to places where they will be most comfortable and where they can see clearly.

Service sheets

Having assembled your guests, they will feel more at ease if they have a programme or order of service. Hymn books, Bibles and prayer books may all be available, but it is often easier if all the relevant information is printed on one sheet. Infrequent church-goers may have difficulty juggling books, so include hymns and any prayers which require a congregational response. For example, in the *Alternative Service Book*, a series of 'acclamations' is often used (section 20, p. 293); it would be helpful to print these with the responses in bold type. Include the names and composers of hymns and of any other musical contributions – people like to know what they are and it is courteous to the composers and musicians.

Copyright

Most churches are covered by Christian Copyright Licensing. You are not allowed to photocopy hymn books but you may copy out the words of hymns and then copy that – as in the case of an order of service. If the wedding venue is not covered by the scheme you may acquire a one-off licence from CCL (see 'Useful Information', p. 157); as most weddings don't usually include more than four hymns, though, it may be quicker to write direct to the copyright holders for permission. Details of the copyright holders and their addresses should be in the hymn book. Similarly, with other pieces of music performed, the organist or musical director should be able to tell you what copyright clearances are required.

Printing

As with the invitations, you can produce the service sheets yourself, adding any graphics which appeal to you. An A4 sheet folded in half should be sufficient, with your names, date and place of service on the front. Don't go for tiny print hoping to fit it all in on a small sheet – this can make for very difficult reading, especially if the church lighting is not the most modern. It is better to use as much paper as you need. In fact, if you know some of your guests have seriously impaired eyesight, or you yourself would prefer not to wear spectacles for your wedding, why not provide some large-print versions?

Recording your wedding

Many couples quite naturally feel they would like a record of their service to look at, listen to or watch in future years. Professional photographers are used to organizing the 'key shots' at weddings, one or two of which may be taken inside the church, such as the signing of the register and the recessional at the end. Anything over and above this tends to be unduly intrusive, though professionals are usually extremely discreet. It is not conducive to the general atmosphere if relatives and friends suddenly start snapping or using camcorders during the service, so deter them if you can. (A note on the service sheet may do the trick, or the church may have some effective but tactful way of doing this.)

Some churches will charge (quite a lot) for the use of a video camera; this is because of copyright regulations. Other churches won't allow a video camera or camcorder at all and it has to be said that a cameraman (or -woman) leaping about is hardly appropriate, especially during the solemn part of the ceremony.

A sound recording of the service (for which there may be a charge) can usually be accommodated unobtrusively if the equipment is available, and is a poignant reminder of your wedding, without the embarrassment of those zoom-shots of Auntie Mary's hat and the spot on the bridesmaid's nose!

At the end of the service

The service is over, you have walked up the aisle, you emerge from the church door – what next? Well, if you're getting married at the height of the season there may well be another wedding waiting to come in soon after yours and you will have been advised of this. You will probably be directed to a part of the churchyard where photographs may be taken. It is a good idea at this stage to have a steward quickly go round the church to make sure nothing has been left, as you won't be able to get back inside immediately. In the register office you may be directed out of a different door to the one you entered by, so your wedding party doesn't get mixed up with the next. The ideal situation is to have the venue to yourselves so there is no rush.

Some churches don't allow confetti and the minister will say something to that effect during the service. Flower petals might be substituted, with permission, in which case you will have to provide them or prime your guests beforehand. One couple emerged to bubbles instead! The stewards issued tins of bubble mixture to key guests and children.

Photographs always seem to take a very long time and people may be standing around awaiting their turn. Make sure elderly people have somewhere to sit down. There may also be a number of people present in church whom you have not invited to the reception or party (in theory anyone can turn up at a wedding because it is a public ceremony). A nice idea is to provide cake (maybe a second, plainer wedding cake) and tea and coffee for those people either at the back of church or in the adjoining church buildings, wherever is most convenient. This always goes down well and people feel included and welcome.

Transport

Couples choose to arrive at church and depart in all sorts of ways, from a horse-drawn carriage or a white Rolls Royce, through to a Harley Davidson or even a tandem! Dare to be different. The main advantage of the bridal couple being driven off on their own afterwards is that they can get a short break before the rest of the celebrations, but if that isn't a priority, why not hire a bus to take everybody to the reception? Don't feel you have to splash out on wedding cars, especially if you live near the church and are not travelling far afterwards. Why not walk to church together, and if you are within walking distance of your reception or party, why not walk there too with all your guests? Then passers-by may have the pleasure of observing the wedding party as well.

The reception

It is not within the brief of this book to advise you about your wedding breakfast, reception, or whatever meal you choose to share with your guests. However, it is worth saying that it is all part of the design of 'the day' and you needn't do the obvious. Some churches have pleasant, well-equipped halls and nothing could be easier than walking a few yards for your reception; a rural church hall often provides a much prettier setting than a formularized hotel. If you are getting married in a hotel or in the grounds of a stately home it makes sense to have it all on site anyway. You could even set the marriage within the context of the meal. If you feel you can trust the weather, eat *al fresco*. If you have room you could take everyone back to your own home, or a relative or friend might be prepared to play host. If your budget is small, don't feel you have to break the bank: the people who care about you just want to be with *you* and enjoy your happiness, they aren't necessarily bothered about whether the food is *cordon bleu*. How about a traditional pie, peas and beer reception? Or cold meat and salad? Or ethnic finger-food? Don't feel tied to a sit-down dinner – a buffet with the opportunity to mingle can be much more relaxed.

Don't feel you have to do the traditional thing in the way of speeches. Many a potential best man has refused the job out of sheer terror of standing up and making a speech! Nowadays there are no hard and fast rules. The bride may want to make a speech, so why shouldn't she? If her father isn't there, her mother might like to take his place; or just bride and groom could speak – it really doesn't matter. It's lovely for someone to propose a toast to the happy couple, though, so best man or chief bridesmaid could do the honours. Be creative! And keep it short; most people aren't used to public speaking and there is nothing worse than somebody you can barely hear, rambling on down the other end of the table!

As time goes on

We have mentioned one or two ideas in Chapter 5 for objects like candles, banners, goblets, etc. being used as symbols during the ceremony and then kept for use at future anniversaries. Some couples like to go back to the church where they were married for a service of re-dedication or thanks on a significant anniversary. A marriage isn't something that happens on one day, it is something that grows and develops with time and it is good to mark and celebrate it. *Human Rites* (Hannah Ward & Jennifer Wild) contains some ideas for services and they are being added to all the time.

Checklist

Items are listed in approximate chronological order. For example, a hotel reception – though the last stop on the day – usually needs to be booked at least a year in advance.

1 Contact Minister or Registrar ○
2 Settle on venue ○
3 Apply for Licence and/or Certificate, or arrange for Banns to be read in all requisite churches ○
4 Decide on personnel:
Best man _____ ○
Chief Bridesmaid/Best woman _____ ○
Other bridesmaids, if any _____ ○
Bride's escort (if any) _____ ○
Stewards/ ushers (2–4) _____ ○
4 Book reception, if necessary ○
5 Print and send invitations; decide about gifts ○
6 The ceremony:
a) ASB or BCP and which options, if marrying in Anglican church ○
Decide format of service if other ○
b) Vows: writing your own? Decide what you want to say. ○

c) Prayers: what would you like? Who will say
   them? ◯

d) Readings:
   Bible reading (i) _____ read by _____ ◯
   Bible reading (ii) _____ read by _____ ◯
   Other _____ read by _____ ◯

e) Music
   Processional accompanist ◯
   Recessional accompanist ◯
   Hymn 1 _____ hymn book _____ ◯
   Hymn 2 _____ hymn book _____ ◯
   Hymn 3 _____ hymn book _____ ◯
   Music during signing of register sung/played by
   _____ ◯
   Any other ◯
   Choir? ◯
   Bells? ◯

f) Organize photographer; video; tape-recording ◯

g) Transport, if any ◯

h) Flowers; banners; any special symbols, for
   example, candles ◯

i) Design and print service sheets and attend to any
   copyright permissions ◯

j) Extras: for example, coffee after the service, who will
   organize and serve? ◯

Appendix 2

Useful Information

Books

Church of England, 'The Marriage Service', *Alternative Service Book*, Central Board of Finance of the Church of England, 1980.

Church of England, 'Matrimony with hymns, Alternative Services', First Series, *Book of Common Prayer*, Cambridge University Press, Oxford University Press, SPCK, 1966.

Church of England, *Services of Prayer and Dedication after Civil Marriage*, Church House Publishing, 1985.

Ross-Macdonald, Jane, *Alternative Weddings*, Thorsons, HarperCollins*Publishers*, 1996.

Magee, Brian CM, *Readings For Your Wedding*, Veritas, 1995.

Read, Charles, *Revising Weddings*, Grove Worship Series 128, 1994.

Ward, Hannah & Wild, Jennifer, *Human Rites: worship resources for an age of change*, Mowbray, 1995.

Further resources

For information on The Family Medallion contact: Clergy
Services, Inc., 706 West 42nd Street, Kansas City, Missouri
64111, USA. tel: (local dial-out code) 1–816–753–3886; Web
address: www.clergyserve.com.; Internet: clergy@tfs.net.

Christian Copyright Licensing, P.O. Box 1339 Eastbourne,
East Sussex BN21 4YF

Acknowledgements

The Anglican Diocese of Christchurch, 'A prayer of forgiveness and healing' from 'An Experimental Liturgy for the Blessing of a Relationship', used with permission.

Bartol, Revd John W., Alternative Introduction and Ceremony of Candles from *The Wedding Ceremony*, reprinted by permission.

The Bible Society, Scriptures quoted from the Good News Bible published by The Bible Societies/HarperCollins *Publishers* Ltd, © American Bible Society 1966, 1971, 1976, 1992, used with permission.

Carmichael, Alexander, 'The peace of God be with you', *Carmina Gadelica*, vol. III, pp. 209, 211, Scottish Academic Press, Edinburgh. Used with kind permission of the trustees of the *Carmina Gadelica*.

Central Board of Finance of the Church of England, extracts from 'The Form of Solemnization of Matrimony', Alternative Services, First Series, 1966, 'The Marriage Service', *Alternative Service Book*, 1980, and *Services of Prayer and Dedication after Civil Marriage*, 1985. Used by permission.

Chisholm, T. O., words of 'Great is Your Faithfulness', version © 1951 Hope Publishing Co. Administered by CopyCare, P. O. Box 77, Hailsham, BN27 3EF, UK. Used by permission.

Acknowledgements

Cobb Anderson, Vienna, 'Parent's Remarriage: as part of the marriage ceremony', © The Revd Vienna Cobb Anderson; used with permission of the Crossroad Publishing Company, New York, NY 10017.

Coleman, Dr Roger, 'Celebrating the Family: a ceremony for recognizing children during the wedding ceremony', © Roger Coleman 1995 and used with permission.

Dudley-Smith, Timothy, words of hymns 'Tell out, my soul' and 'Lord, for the years', © Hope Publishing Co. in the United States and Canada. Reprinted with permission.

Edlin-White, Rowena, 'Wedding Day', and 'Love', © Rowena Edlin-White 1996.

Edwards, Clare, 'On the Occasion of a Second Marriage', © D. Clare Edwards, and used with permission.

Eliot, T. S., 'A Dedication to My Wife', from *Collected Poems 1909–1962*, T. S. Eliot, reprinted by permission of Faber & Faber Ltd; copyright 1936 by Harcourt Brace & Company, © 1964, 1963, by T. S. Eliot, reprinted with permission of the publisher.

Green, Donald A., 'Love is the will to nurture', and Penn, William, 'Never marry but for love', from *Quaker Faith and Practice 1994*; reprinted by permission of the Religious Society of Friends.

Gibran, Kahlil, extracts from *The Prophet*, Copyright 1923 by Kahlil Gibran and renewed 1951 by Administrators CTA of Kahlil Gibran Estate and Mary G. Gibran. Reprinted by permission of Alfred A. Knopf Inc.

Gurney, Dorothy F., 'O perfect love', words by Dorothy F. Gurney (1858–1932) (this version Words & Music/Jubilate Hymns) © Oxford University Press; used by permission.

Idle, Christopher, 'Commemoration', from *Prayers for the People*, ed. Michael Perry, Marshall Pickering, 1982, reprinted with permission.

Jamieson, Morley, 'The Birthday', from *Scottish Love Poems*, Antonia Fraser, Cannongate Publishing Ltd, 1975.

Jenkins, David, 'A time to love ... and a time to hate' from *Further Everyday Prayers*, ed. Helen Snashall, National Christian Education Council, 1992.

Johnson, Malcolm, extract from 'A Service of Blessing' from *Human Rites*, Hannah Ward and Jennifer Wild, Mowbray, 1995, reprinted with permission.

Jubilate Hymns, words of hymns 'All creatures of our God and king', 'Bring to the Lord a glad new song', 'Great is your faithfulness', 'Come down, O Love divine!', 'Love divine, all loves excelling', 'May the mind of Christ my saviour', 'Lord Jesus Christ', 'O God beyond all praising', 'O perfect love', and 'The king of love my shepherd is' reprinted with permission.

L'Engle, Madeleine, extract from *The Irrational Season* published by HarperCollins New York, NY 10022, © 1977. Used with permission.

Mackenzie, Compton, 'Bridal Day' from *Scottish Love Poems*, Antonia Fraser, Cannongate Publishing Ltd. Used with permission of The Society of Authors as the Literary Representative of the Estate of Compton Mackenzie.

Milne, Don, prayers from *Our Marriage Book*.

Muir, Edwin, 'The Confirmation', from *The Collected Poems*, Edwin Muir, Oxford University Press, 1960; copyright © 1960 by Edwin Muir. Used by permission of Oxford University Press, Inc., and Faber & Faber Ltd.

Nash, Ogden, 'Reprise', from *Versus*, published by J. M. Dent & Sons Ltd, 1956. Reprinted by permission of Curtis Brown Ltd. Copyright © 1949 by Ogden Nash.

'God of tenderness and strength' from 'The Marriage Service', *A New Zealand Prayer Book*.

Acknowledgements

NIV, Scripture quotations taken from the HOLY BIBLE, NEW INTERNATIONAL VERSION®. NIV® Copyright © 1973, 1978, 1984 by International Bible Society. Used by permission of Zondervan Publishing House. All rights reserved. 'NIV' is a registered trademark of International Bible Society. UK trademark number 1448790.

NRSV, quotations are from the New Revised Standard Version Apocryphal/Deuterocanonical Books, Copyright 1989 by the Division of Christian Education of the National Council of the Churches of Christ in the USA. Used by permission. All rights reserved.

Perry, Michael, Prayer for a Newly-Married Couple, About Belonging, For Every Day, For Our Future, For the Remarried, About Belonging, Blessings from Psalms 115 & 128, from *Prayers for the People*, ed. Michael Perry, Marshall Pickering, 1992, used with permission; also words to hymns 'Bring to the Lord a glad new song', 'O God beyond all praising', and 'Lord Jesus Christ' © Michael Perry/ Jubilate Hymns.

Peterson, Robert J., adaptation of 'Prayers for the Bride and Groom' from *A Marriage Service for You*, reprinted by permission from CSS Publishing Company Inc., 517 S. Main St., PO Box 4503, Lima, Ohio 45802–4503, USA.

Scovell, E. J., 'Marriage and Death' from *Collected Poems*, Carcanet Press Ltd, 1988, reprinted with permission.

Teilhard de Chardin, Pierre, extract from *The Hymn of the Universe*, Collins, © HarperCollins New York, 1965. Used with permission.

United Reformed Church, The Wedding Service, section 8, from *The Service Book of The United Reformed Church in the United Kingdom*, Oxford University Press, 1989, reprinted with permission.

Weil, Simone, extract from *Waiting on God*, Fontana Books, 1973. Reprinted by permission of HarperCollins*Publishers*.

Williams, Dick, 'Wedding Day' from *More Prayers for Today's Church*, Kingsway, 1984, reprinted with permission; 'For the Bereaved' from *Prayers for the People*, ed. Michael Perry, Marshall Pickering, 1982. Used with permission.

Index by Author